An Accidental Triumph

The Improbable

History of American

Higher Education

Sol Gittleman

Vesto
Books

Published 2023 by Vesto Books
P.O. Box 118
Ringoes, NJ 08551

Printed in the United States of America

ISBN: 9781959000044 (paperback)
ELECTRONIC ISBN: 9781959000051 (ebook)

A version of the preface previously appeared in
The Chronicle of Higher Education in 2015 as
"Higher Education Has Always Been a Mess:
That's what makes it great"

Our distributor offers special discounts for bulk
purchases by organizations and institutions.
A reading group guide is also available. Please contact
vestobooks@proton.me for more information.

Library of Congress Control Number: 2023931530

Edited by Phil Primack

*Copyediting and corrections by Fred Kameny, Alison Rooney,
Caitlin Solano, and Patsy Wang-Iverson*

*Cover and interior design by Amanda Weiss
Cover art: Diploma © Arcady / Adobe Stock;
darts © StockVector / Adobe Stock*

*Special thanks to Sara Georgi, Natalie Homer,
Derek Krissoff, Sarah Munroe, and Than Saffel*

FSC
www.fsc.org
MIX
Paper from
responsible sources
FSC® C005010

To Jeremy and Phil,
who made it happen

Contents

A History Like No Other

"A peculiar combination of historical circumstances shaped the American system of higher education, like a benevolent Providence, turning its negative features—fragmentation, incoherence, qualitative unevenness, and economic vulnerability—almost into assets."

—HUGH DAVIS GRAHAM AND NANCY DIAMOND,
The Rise of American Research Universities[1]

This is a book about how Americans regard higher education: what they think of our colleges and universities. It is a personal view, documented and characterized by my own lifelong experiences as a student and teacher.

Imagine archaeologists digging through the remains of our civilization five hundred years from now. They will find signs of political dysfunction and social inequity, and would likely conclude that three key factors shaped America's fate as a global force. The first was the application, successful and otherwise, of America's enormous military might around the world. The second was

---

1. (Baltimore: Johns Hopkins University Press, 2004), 125.

no-holds-barred creative capitalism, which drove America's global dominance—until it no longer did. But the apparent third factor would confuse the cultural detectives from the twenty-sixth century: According to the fragments of surviving documents, American leadership around the world was eventually undermined by a sclerotic higher educational system of thousands of ungovernable colleges and universities.

Take, for example, an official government document titled *A Nation at Risk*, dated 1983, that stated, "If an unfriendly foreign power had attempted to impose on America the mediocre educational performance that exists today, we might well have viewed it as an act of war." Was there really a conspiracy to destroy the United States from within its academic institutions? Why did the author, William Bennett, feel he had to write this piece to warn uninformed citizens that their colleges and universities were contributing to the destruction of the American dream?

But there is a far different story about American higher education. In this infrequent and scarcely documented telling, America created, mostly by accident and rarely by design, a higher education enterprise unlike anything in the world. Even as a torrent of American-authored books was predicting an academic Armageddon and failure on a cosmic scale, an unprecedented Golden Age in the post–World War II century made American higher education the envy of the world. Envied, that is, except in the United States itself.

Entire forests have been sacrificed in the last fifty years to produce books about our colleges and universities. In this one, I hope to offer some perspective on this stark contrast between worldwide admiration and national disapproval. With four centuries of American higher education to examine, some context might help a curious and confused reader to understand today's headlines lamenting the crippling student debt, admissions scandals, predatory sexual abuses by faculty, a nationwide gambling-fueled athletic system that exploits student participants, and an endowment-driven hunt for anyone's donor dollars that has corrupted the chase for philanthropic support. And that's before getting to criticism of mediocre teaching, research fraud, and ideological dishonesty.

A century ago, no one would have predicted the current state of fault-finding in the national dialogue. In the years immediately after World War I, inward-looking Americans had no shortage of other targets at which to aim their scorn: European chaos fueled by new ideologies, a porous American immigration policy that let in undesirables who threatened to add to racial and political unrest, animus toward foreigners in general, and the aftermath of a ravaging pandemic, the name-blaming "Spanish Flu." But observers of America's difficulties rarely mentioned our colleges or universities.

Not so today. Beyond our borders, almost universal appreciation exists for this enormous, flawed, and disorganized academic enterprise that America has created.

Until the COVID-19 pandemic disrupted the world economy, the United States had a $36 *billion* trade surplus in
higher education, with a million international students
populating our campuses.[2] Still, many American poli-
ticians, journalists, and even members of our own profession see American colleges and universities as failing
in just about everything. Hardly a day passes without
reference to some scandal, fraud, intellectual or moral
failure, or other ill associated with American academic
institutions. Worldwide admiration and continued American dominance of the Nobel Prizes seem to make no
difference.

My goal is to help the non-specialist, the puzzled and
confused American confronted by the public debate
about the status and quality of our colleges and universities. If American higher education is such a failure, why
are students and scholars from all over the world still so
eager to secure a place in one of these institutions? Why
do American faculty dominate the worldwide compe-
titions in research every year? What are we—a higher
education disaster or the envy of the world? The brief
answer is—both.

2. The National Center for Education Statistics provides a number of
more than 4,500 for universities and colleges in this country, but often
does not include branch or satellite locations, for-profit institutions approved by the Accrediting Commission of Career Schools and Colleges,
or many of the hundreds of Bible colleges listed by national faith-related
accrediting organizations, such as the Association for Biblical Higher
Education, the Association of Advanced Rabbinical and Talmud Schools,
and the Association of Independent Christian Colleges and Seminaries.

The following chapters, I hope, will help explain this paradox and provide a chronological story that describes the evolution of our post-secondary institutions from their most modest beginnings, the impact of religion and race, the expansion of the nation, the unique character of private philanthropy in the American tradition, the peculiar limitations we imposed on ourselves in the first half of the twentieth century, and then the unforeseen "accident" initiated by a leader of another country that resulted in the death of millions, worldwide destruction, and the displacement of people to the eventual benefit of the United States.

For more than half a century, I have been an eyewitness of and participant in this authentically "exceptional" American experience. Without planning, I was preparing for this even earlier.

My first impression of college goes back to my childhood in 1940s Hoboken, New Jersey, the child of East European immigrants who did not read or write English. My exposure to American higher education was through the movies, where I took my Yiddish-speaking grandmother three times a week, preferably to see anything with the Marx Brothers, including their 1932 movie *Horse Feathers*. My first image of an American college president was Groucho Marx as Quincy Adams Wagstaff, the new leader of Huxley College, who thought he was recruiting two professional football players—brothers Harpo and Chico—to help his school win "The Big Game" against rival Darwin College. An older, mature, and attractive non-student female hanging around the team led Zeppo Marx into dangerous waters. I couldn't wait to go to college.

My other vivid encounter with higher education was *Knute Rockne, All-American* (1940), which converted me and other Jewish boys into rabid supporters of Pat O'Brien and Notre Dame, always ready to "win one for the Gipper," the immortal Fighting Irish halfback George Gipp, played in the movie by future President Ronald Reagan. A few other campus-based football movies and Mickey Rooney as Andy Hardy going off to college established the expectations of most Americans. If average mid-twentieth-century Americans thought at all about college or university, they were more likely concerned with the outcome of the New Year's Rose Bowl football game than with anything connected to academic excellence.

But events during the decades just before and after World War II led to an unimagined postwar surge by this nation's colleges and universities, driven by the actions of foreign governments and the consequences of unforeseen domestic policy decisions. Like the geological crash of continents, American educational accomplishment and university-based research achievement were forced upward at an unprecedented speed to the top of the world, *and there we have remained*.

How did it happen? The record and the evidence take us on a winding journey that goes back to colonial American roots.

In seventeenth-century colonial America, a mandatory religious orthodoxy dominated the small number of campuses and college communities: Harvard was for the Congregationalists, Yale for the Calvinists. Often, it was a matter of life and death. Quakers were being hanged on the Boston Common. Baptists were drowned on the banks of the Charles River before fleeing to Providence, where they founded a college named after their benefactor, Nicholas Brown Jr. Evangelical Presbyterians left for New Jersey to await the coming of the Messiah, and to create a college later named Princeton. In the Virginia colony, the Anglicans had the College of William & Mary. Higher education completely identified with a white Protestant American theocracy, staffed by a handful of poorly trained teachers whose purpose was to prepare future ministers of their own faith and, when necessary, to maintain order. When Thomas Jefferson established the more liberal University of Virginia, with the first class enrolled in 1825, the faculty slept with loaded pistols under their pillows for fear of being murdered in their sleep by riotous students.[3]

Up to the time of the Civil War, the United States was peppered with dozens of denominationally Baptist, Methodist, Lutheran, Presbyterian, and other faith-based colleges throughout the eastern states and Midwestern frontier territories serving the evangelical hopes of their founders and bringing Christianity to the "heathens." For those Irish Catholics who poured into the New World

---

3. See Rex Bowman and Carlos Santos, *Rot, Riot, and Rebellion: Mr. Jefferson's Struggle to Save the University That Changed America* (Charlottesville: University of Virginia Press, 2013).

after the 1840s, Georgetown, Holy Cross, and Boston College would serve in the East, while Notre Dame, founded in 1842, followed Catholic settlers into the territories. Memoirs and diaries speak of mediocre teachers and a generally impractical curriculum that had changed little from the time of classical antiquity. If one was serious about rigorous education, there was only one place to go: Europe.

Two key developments changed the educational landscape in the nineteenth-century United States. The first was the Morrill Land Grant Acts of 1862 and 1890, which emphasized vocational and applied training as well as defense of the nation. The other was the rise of philanthropic industrialists with names such as Rockefeller, Vanderbilt, Hopkins, Stanford, Duke, Carnegie, and Mellon, who wanted German-style research universities and put their money to work.[4]

However, no one could catch the Germans, whose state-controlled, centralized academic-industrial collaboration led the rest of the world. Any doubts about German worldwide leadership in scientific research ended when the Nobel Prizes began in 1901. The science awards looked like a wholly owned German subsidiary.

As the twentieth century began, the United States might have been able to mount a challenge, but when a defeated Germany was at its most vulnerable after World

4. See chapter 8, "The German Influence," 367–412, in Richard Hofstadter and Walter P. Metzger, *The Development of Academic Freedom in the United States* (New York: Columbia University Press, 1955).

War I, nativist sentiments led to changes in American immigration policies that shut the doors. Earlier, masses of southern and eastern European immigrants had poured into the United States after 1880, fleeing poverty in Italy and chaos in Russia. Once settled in the New World, many were eager for their children to pursue higher education. These Jewish and Italian immigrants produced an abundance of offspring, and as the century turned to the 1900s, the now college-age first generation was ready to storm the campuses. They met academic and social resistance from biologists and American nativists, whose fear of racial pollution argued for a national policy of restrictive immigration.

For most Americans growing up in the 1930s and 1940s, college and university meant football, fraternities, comical absent-minded professors, and an all-white student body manufactured in Hollywood that had as little to do with intellectual life as possible. For many of us with immigrant parents, living as I did in one room behind my father's candy store and attending the local public schools, those campuses might have well as been on a different planet. Our teachers told the few of us applying to college which schools would accept us; no one from my high school graduating class applied to what we call today an Ivy League institution. "Prestige" was a meaningless word in any college selection conversation, having significance only if a neighbor drove a Buick or Chrysler, instead of a Chevrolet or Plymouth.

World War II and its aftermath—most significantly the emigration to the United States of refugee scholars, researchers, and scientists who would reshape the American college and university—changed everything, permanently. Fortunately for me, I became part of the second phase of that historic change, one of the children of immigrants who, because of the enormous number of returning veterans, found opportunity where previously none had existed. My generation of academics was the luckiest in history. We entered the profession in the 1950s, when deans were desperate to find anyone with a Ph.D. and a pulse, whether scientist, social scientist, or humanist. We were needed to stand or sit in front of the exploding numbers of undergraduates and graduate students filling the campuses in the decades after World War II, when there were simply not enough faculty available. That postwar era had few formal tenure reviews, little outside expert opinion on candidates' qualifications for a permanent appointment, and few strict publication requirements. Positions were available from California to New England, from Washington State to Florida, at colleges and universities small or large, public or private. At the same time, twenty years after the end of World War II, American higher education, as measured by its research accomplishments and extraordinary diversity of campuses, had attained unaccustomed eminence in the eyes of the world.

I was not trained as a historian, and this is not intended to be a book by an expert for other scholars of American higher education. Nor is this a "how to fix" or "how to disrupt" analysis that offers a pathway to change or survival. Rather, I am writing for the interested reader who lacks the time, inclination, or preparation to read any of the countless documents chronicling the unscripted evolution of American colleges and universities. That narrative is available, but not even the most dedicated nonprofessional reader could tackle, for example, the 521 small-font, four-column, tightly packed pages of academic essays and essential primary sources in the single, colossal volume of *American Higher Education Transformed, 1940–2005: Documenting the National Discourse*.[5]

I am indebted to a group of eminent historians of higher education: Bryan Alexander, James Axtell, Thomas Bender, Derek Bok, William Bowen, David Breneman, Steven Brint, Jonathan Cole, Nancy Diamond, Roger L. Geiger, Hugh Davis Graham, Mary and Oscar Handlin, Richard Hofstadter, William C. Kirby, Adam Laats, David F. Labaree, Emily J. Levine, Christopher Loss, Christopher J. Lucas, Walter Metzger, Henry Rosovsky, Frederick Rudolph, Wilson Smith, John K. Thelin, Martin Trow, Laurence Veysey, Jonathan Zimmerman, and others cited. I am not one of their number. But as a participant for more than sixty years in the higher education world that they study, I have seen much.

5. Ed. Thomas H. Bender and Wilson Smith (Baltimore: Johns Hopkins University Press, 2008).

CHAPTER ONE

In the Beginning

The First 200 Years

"It is ordered that if any Student of this College shall deny the being of a God, the existence of Virtue & Vice, or that the books of the Old and New Testament are of divine authority, or suggest any scruples of that nature, or circulate books of such pernicious tendency; or frequent the company of those who are known to favour such fatal errors, or harrass and disquiet the minds of his fellow Students, respecting any of the peculiarities of their Christian faith by ridicule, sneers, scoffing infidel Suggestions, or in any other way; and shall continue obstinate therein after the first & second admonition, he shall be expelled from the College."

— *The Laws of the College in Providence in the State of Rhode Island, Enacted by the Fellowship and Approved by the Trustees of Sd. College,* 1783

The first two hundred years of American higher education were marked by: various degrees of sectarian theocracy, exclusion of almost everyone except white male youth of a certain economic standing, low academic standards, and the failure of most of the colleges that had opened their doors.[1] The historian Donald Tewksbury claimed that of the 516 colleges and universities that had established themselves in the eighteenth and nineteenth century Pennsylvania, New York, Ohio, Virginia, North Carolina, Maryland, Alabama, Tennessee, Georgia, Louisiana, Missouri, Mississippi, Texas, Kansas, Florida, and Arkansas, 412 had failed by the time the first shot was fired at Fort Sumter in 1861, setting off the Civil War. The most optimistic view placed the failure rate at one in five.[2] With few exceptions—Thomas Jefferson's University of Virginia being the most prominent—almost all the survivors were faith-based extensions of Protestant religious denominations. The "College in Providence" described earlier eventually became Brown University, though in its earliest form it was created for Baptist exiles who had fled Boston's religious persecutions to find sanctuary and avoid the fate of the Quakers on the hanging trees of the Boston Common. For some college graduates, it continued to be a matter of life and death, as several of the accusers and accused discovered in 1693 in Salem, Massachusetts, where Harvard College was represented by both judges and alleged disciples of the Devil. Much as Jefferson had tried to abandon a religious

1. Donald G. Tewksbury, *The Founding of American Colleges and Universities before the Civil War* (New York: Teachers College Bureau of Publications, 1932), 28. Recent historians suggest that Tewksbury's figures are exaggerated, but all agree that the failure rates were enormous.

2. James Axtell, *Wisdom's Workshop: The Rise of the Modern University* (Princeton: Princeton University Press, 2015), 162.

test in Virginia, even the state universities retained one of some sort. The University of Georgia charter (1785) states: "All Officers appointed to the instruction, and government of the University, shall be of the Christian Religion."[3] From the outset, American colleges were subject to the forces of an imposed conformity—today's "political correctness"—as well as the marketplace; you could start a sectarian college overnight, but if you didn't attract students, you disappeared just as quickly.

The earliest attendees, those young men who eventually would fill the earliest Harvard College seats, reflected the class system brought to the colonies by the leaders of the Boston settlement in the 1630s. In association with the clergy, this was seventeenth-century Boston aristocracy. Governor John Winthrop had made it clear that the Massachusetts Bay Colony and its earliest academic institution were an extension of natural law: "In all times some must be rich, some poore, some highe and eminent in power and dignitie; others meane and in subjection."[4]

These first institutions of higher learning might have been modeled in some abstract fashion on Oxford and Cambridge in the mother country, but they lacked any of the characteristics that produced the great European universities in the Italian and German states and later in the Netherlands from the twelfth to the seventeenth

3. See John R. Thelin, *Essential Documents in the History of American Higher Education* (Baltimore: Johns Hopkins University Press), 44.

4. John Winthrop, *A Modell of Christian Charity*, https://history.hanover.edu/texts/winthmod.html.

century. From the time of the founding of the first college, Harvard in 1636, to 1769 there were a total of just nine tiny institutions in the American colonies: Harvard, William & Mary, Yale, Princeton, Columbia, Pennsylvania, Brown, Rutgers, and Dartmouth. Collectively they produced fewer than two hundred graduates a year. Their primary task was to prepare clergy for their calling and to maintain a semblance of discipline. The ability to preach faith and to maintain order were the only qualifications necessary for the poorly paid and untrained faculty. As for college preparation, it did not exist in any systematic way. There would be no standard secondary education for several centuries, not even for the elites who generally made up the small student bodies. The historian Jill Lepore characterized the state of American higher education: "Before the Civil War, most American colleges were evangelical, college presidents were ministers, and every branch of scholarship was guided by religion."[5]

The first great expansion of higher educational institutions occurred after the Revolutionary War during a reinvigorated religious revival in the former colonies that moved westward with settlers. If there had been any doubt that the United States would remain a profoundly Christian country, it was made clear by the religious activities

5. *These Truths* (New York: W. W. Norton, 2018), 348. From its origins and through the centuries, evangelical and millennial forces were never far from the center of American thought. See Ernest R. Sandeen, *The Roots of Fundamentalism: British and American Millenarianism, 1800–1930* (Chicago: University of Chicago Press, 1970); George M. Marsden, *Fundamentalism and American Culture*, 2nd edition (New York: Oxford University Press, 2006).

associated with what historians have identified as the second Great Awakening in what was by then the United States of America. The number of clergymen grew from eighteen hundred in 1775 to nearly forty thousand by 1845. As the frontier moved west into the Appalachians and beyond, religious millenarian fervor went with it and led to an explosion of new colleges identified, among many other Protestant sects, by their Methodist, Baptist, Lutheran, and Presbyterian evangelicalism. Christ was coming to the frontier, and the new colleges would carry his flag.[6] Regardless of the denominational identity, the colleges shared an acceptance of Harvard College's earliest mottos: "Christo et Ecclesiae" and "In Christi Gloriam." Thomas Jefferson and Benjamin Franklin might be counted among the fathers of a nation that proclaimed the separation of church and state, but as they pushed westward, the founders of the American colleges placed Jesus Christ at the very center of their educational mission, even if they argued about which denomination should carry the banner.[7] Often the evangelical zeal took

6. For the links between this American historical past and modern Christian colleges and universities, see Manning M. Pattillo Jr. and Donald M. Mackenzie, *Church-Sponsored Higher Education in the United States: Report of the Danforth Commission* (Washington: American Council on Education, 1966); and Samuel Schuman, *Seeing the Light: American Religious Colleges in Twenty-First-Century America* (Baltimore: Johns Hopkins University Press, 2010). Also, Jurgen Herbst, *From Crisis to Crisis: American College Government, 1636–1819* (Cambridge: Harvard University Press, 1982). For expansion of clergymen, see Alan Taylor, *American Revolutions: A Continental History, 1750–1804* (New York: W. W. Norton, 2016), 444–52.

7. "As the evangelical tide swept westward, it became clear that the religious conquest of America was mainly in the hands of three

the form of "a mission to the savages." Native inhabitants became the target for conversion in the eyes of these frontier Christian education apostles. Many of the new colleges saw it as their Christian mission to bring faith to the "heathens," and with the expansion of the United States by the Louisiana Purchase in 1803, hundreds of frontier colleges appeared as if overnight. Many disappeared just as quickly. Of the twenty colleges that opened in Kansas in the years leading up to the North-South conflict, all but one had closed before the attack on Fort Sumter. In Texas, thirty-eight out of forty did not survive.[8] "Colleges rise like mushrooms in our luxurious soil," an eyewitness noted in 1829. "They are duly lauded and puffed for a day, and then they sink to be heard of no more."[9] The historian John Thelin, looking back from the twenty-first century, described the risks: "The motto for a group seeking to found a new college [during the first half of the nineteenth century] might have been translated into English as 'Good Luck—and Fat Chance!'"[10] The colleges failed for a variety of reasons: denominational competition, financial distress, internal religious and political dissension, poor location, natural disaster (dozens burned to the ground, some to be rebuilt only to again be destroyed by fire). Disease could wipe out

---

denominations: the Methodists, the Baptists, and the Presbyterians." Richard Hofstadter, *Anti-Intellectualism in American Life* (New York: Alfred A. Knopf, 1962), Vintage edition, 90.

8. Tewksbury, *The Founding of American Colleges and Universities*, 28.

9. Tewksbury, *The Founding of American Colleges and Universities*, 24.

10. Thelin, *Essential Documents*, 41.

an educational community; epidemics of smallpox and malaria could consume entire settlements, along with the colleges they supported.

If there were not enough qualified faculty for the small number of students at the original nine campuses, one could imagine the level of instruction on the hundreds of new start-up frontier campuses in the eighteenth and early nineteenth centuries. Clergy and laymen with or without formal or even secondary school training were pressed into service as instructors, not only in the colleges but also in hundreds of institutions that passed for medical and law schools.[11] Credentials from these institutions gave no promise of competency. The only thing that counted was faith.

Unlike in Europe, pre–Civil War American colleges and universities were inconsequential in the development of the nation. The historian Laurence Veysey noted that "colleges were really irrelevant, they played no role in shaping society or making change."[12] Few seemed to care, other than the clergy, since the colleges were the primary producer of ministers. Amherst College, founded in 1821, produced 106 graduates in its first six classes:

11. Colin B. Burke, *American Collegiate Populations* (New York: NYU Press, 1982), 319–29. There were estimated to be over 150 medical schools in the United States before the Civil War, mostly proprietary, for-profit, and non-regulated. There were at least 50 law schools that called themselves by that name. There were no educational requirements for admission. Thelin estimates the number of mostly free-standing medical schools at 175. See also John R. Thelin, *A History of Higher Education* (Baltimore: Johns Hopkins University Press, 2004), 53.

12. Laurence Veysey, *The Emergence of the American University* (Chicago: University of Chicago Press, 1965), 9.

68 accepted appointments with various churches. Dartmouth's first ten classes after its establishment in 1769 produced 99 graduates, of whom 46 became clergymen. Any suggestion that somehow this period could provide the foundation for a future Golden Age was dismissed by Roger Geiger: "The first decades of the nineteenth century marked a low point in all the vital signs of American higher education. It had become ineffective in promoting culture, careers, or knowledge."[13] As the century progressed, there was no indication that higher education institutions in the United States were improving. Samuel Eliot Morison, in his official history of Harvard College, wrote: "Almost every graduate of the period 1825–1869 has left on record his detestation of the system of instruction at Harvard."[14]

And despite the religious dedication found among some of the undergraduates and faculty, many of the campuses that survived were in a constant state of chaos and drink-induced disorder. At Harvard, even with its compulsory chapel attendance, 43 of the 70 seniors awaiting graduation were expelled for rioting before commencement in 1823.[15] It was the rare campus community that didn't suffer some student uprising or student-led violence. In the South, dueling with sword or pistol was

13. *The History of American Higher Education: Learning and Culture from the Founding to World War II* (Princeton: Princeton University Press, 2015), 542.

14. Quoted in *The American College in the Nineteenth Century*, Roger L. Geiger (Ed.), (Nashville: Vanderbilt University Press, 2000), 89.

15. Frederick Rudolph, *The American College and University: A History* (New York: Alfred A. Knopf, 1962), 118.

a normal event. Presidents were pistol-whipped and faculty routinely beaten.

By 1815, thirty-three colleges had managed to survive, but the nation's future seemed, to the ordinary American, disconnected from the academic curriculum. "Who wants Latin or Greek or abstruse mathematics in a country like this?" one North Carolina property owner asked.[16] The overwhelming majority of Americans would have agreed. If any American were serious about his further education, he set his eyes on Europe, where the German universities had already attained a position atop the academic world. They had created a new degree and a new vision for the growth of intellectual attainment at the beginning of the industrial nineteenth century: a research degree, the Ph.D., on which a soon-to-be unified German Reich would begin to build its economic and military strength. In the first half of the nineteenth century, nothing could be further from the hope for higher education in the United States. When Chancellor Otto von Bismarck became the leader of a single German empire in 1871, he found a university system fully dedicated to the cause and to celebrating the nation. As for America, the education historian Martin Trow described the state of affairs: "Until after the Civil War, whatever the United States called its institutions of higher learning, it did not have a single genuine university— an institution of first-class standing, that could bring

16. Quoted in Gordon Wood, *Empire of Liberty* (New York: Oxford University Press, 2009), 472.

its students as far or as deep into the various branches of learning as could the institutions of the old world . . . We have offered Europeans nearly two centuries of innocent amusement at our expense."[17]

17. "American Higher Education: Past, Present, and Future," *Educational Researcher*, vol. 17, no. 3 (1988), 16.

CHAPTER TWO

Transformation of Sorts

1860–1900

"It required but the briefest examination to show that amongst the thousand institutions in English-speaking North America which bore the name college or university there was little unity of purpose or of standards. A large majority bearing the name were really concerned with secondary education."

—ABRAHAM FLEXNER, 1910[1]

SENATOR MORRILL AND HIS ACTS

Since the U.S. Constitution made no provisions for a federal role in higher education, states and territories were responsible for their own rules, regulations, and standards. As settlers moved through the Appalachian mountain gaps and continued westward, the approximately 250 colleges and universities that they established

---

1. *Medical Education in the United States and Canada: A Report to the Carnegie Foundation for the Advancement of Teaching, Bulletin No. 4.*

reflected, right up to the start of the American Civil War, the regional educational standards of the nation. Ohio's thirty-seven colleges were exclusively denominational. Any church or minister in either state or territory could announce a new college or seminary and receive authority to grant degrees, with a president in charge. He might also be the only faculty member, though perhaps supplemented by a few ministers teaching some Bible or Gospel and whatever Greek or Latin they might possess. Even in the older institutions of the East, the president had the final word, and that word derived from the Almighty. When Yale's Timothy Dwight was faced with the recommendation that an honorary degree be awarded in 1798 to Edward Jenner, the discoverer of the smallpox vaccine, he refused to approve, announcing that "if God had decreed from all eternity that a certain person should die of smallpox, it would be a frightful sin to void and annul that decree by the trick of vaccination."[2] Jenner, later described as the father of immunology, did not receive his Yale honorary degree. Presidential authority and theological orthodoxy continued to govern higher education in America.

But as the frontier pushed westward, the settlers saw a need for a helping hand with more practical assistance than the faith-driven colleges could provide. Between the Revolutionary and Civil wars, as many as 700 colleges had already failed, many in the new territories. Their

2. Marvin E. Bryce, *Challenge to the Church* (Bloomington, Ind.: Author House, 2005), 77.

curriculum, based in classical languages and the Bible, offered little assistance to a local constituency either trying to squeeze a living out of the land or starting up a modest manufacturing enterprise without experience or advice, still in sight of a hostile frontier often occupied by native inhabitants who had no intention of giving up their land to the interlopers. Military training thus became another much-needed subject. Legislators and academics from Illinois and Michigan were actively lobbying before the outbreak of hostilities for the creation of some sort of agricultural college funded by state or territory. In 1855 the Agricultural College of the State of Michigan was signed into law by the state legislators.

Two years earlier an effort had been started in Illinois to establish a federal program to create industrial colleges aimed at encouraging manufacture in all the states. But the nation's political power still lay in the former eastern colonies, and as a strategy, the midwestern legislators thought that an eastern state politician would have more influence and credibility for legislation that would be funded by federal act. The money for these institutions would come from grants of federal land to be sold or managed by the state government.

Hovering in the immediate background was always the question of slavery and race. The impetus for the legislation came from slave-free states in the North; that was enough to raise the suspicions of the southern states, which were always on the lookout for expanded federal authority. The Illinois delegation, seeking a reliable eastern sponsor, looked to the northern legislators. When they settled on Representative Justin Morrill of Vermont to introduce the bill, there was also assurance of immediate southern opposition to any education bill that permitted the races to mingle. Still, Morrill enthusiastically endorsed the legislation. The son of a blacksmith, he thought that education should also be available for the children of farmers and others who labored with their hands. He rewrote the Illinois version in which each state received the same grant of land so that federal land was ceded to the states on the basis of population: thirty thousand acres of federal land for each senator and congressman, with the sale of this land providing funds for the establishment of these "colleges for agriculture and mechanical arts." But Morrill's bill was vetoed after it passed and went to President James Buchanan in 1857. Buchanan, generally acknowledged by historians as one of the nation's most inept presidents, supported the southern position that this was an unconstitutional federal intrusion into states' rights.

After the outbreak of hostilities between the states, Morrill reintroduced his bill in 1861 to a now exclusively northern Congress. It again set aside the thirty thousand acres of federal lands as a grant, based on the number of congressmen and senators, for immediate or later use or sale, the profits of which would support the new "land-grant" universities. The bill made the purpose of these institutions clear: an emphasis on teaching the latest means and methods of agriculture, which were also called the "mechanical arts" of manufacture—the beginnings of what later became the technology of engineering—and "military tactics" that would focus on the defense of the nation.[3] If the administration wanted to maintain some commitment to the classical curriculum, that was permitted, as long as it was understood that the purpose of a land-grant education was practical and vocational, aimed at agriculture and manufacture.[4] President Lincoln signed the bill into law on July 2, 1862. This was the beginning of a federal initiative, ceded to the states to implement, that eventually led to the transfer of more than seventeen million acres to the states to be used exclusively for public higher education. Vocationalism and practical education were now permanently embedded in post-secondary studies.

3. From this moment on, all land-grant institutions were required to offer military instruction, right through the Reserve Officer Training Corps (ROTC) programs of the modern era. Antiwar faculty votes at land-grant institutions had no effect. The law was clear: maintain military training or close. The anti–Vietnam War faction at land-grant MIT during that conflict was aware that resolutions to close ROTC were futile.

4. This was the beginning of the great "A&M" (agricultural and mechanical) state university system, which profoundly affected the plains and western states. Iowa and Kansas had the first state legislatures to pass land-grant resolutions during the Civil War, and within a few years after the end of hostilities, new state universities appeared in Nebraska, Colorado, Wyoming, South and North Dakota, Texas, and Oklahoma. In some states, an earlier state university with a more classical tradition maintained a separate existence on a different campus (Kansas, Oklahoma, Texas, Colorado, South Dakota, Iowa). Other states combined their two institutions on one campus (Nebraska and Wyoming). Today we have large university communities in cities across these states, each sometimes described as an "A&M" or "State" university, or simply as the "University of . . . ." See Ames and Iowa City, Iowa; East Lansing and Ann Arbor, Michigan; College Station and Austin, Texas; Manhattan and Lawrence, Kansas, among many others.

There was also at least a gesture regarding gender and race in the language of Senator Morrill's legislation. Women and Black people were technically permitted to enroll in these northern schools. Tuition would be free to all, as well as a stipend for transportation to and from the farms. But even in the North, inequality was a way of life. Only three northern states—Massachusetts, Maine, and New Hampshire—had permitted full Black voting rights. The Lincoln-Douglas debates reflected how white-majority America viewed the Black population, free or slave. In the Fourth Debate of September 18, 1858, Stephen Douglas spoke for most white Americans, North and South: "I say that this Government was established on the white basis. It was made for white men, for the benefit of white men and their posterity forever, and never should be administered by any except white men. I declare that a negro ought not to be a citizen . . . he is a negro, belonging to a race incapable of self-government, and for that reason ought not to be on any equality with white men." There was immense applause.[5] The debate was held in Charleston, Illinois, the size of its audience boosted by wagons filled with out-of-state Indiana Douglas sympathizers in attendance. How much opportunity Black students would have in these land-grant public universities was anyone's guess, but even northern legislators made it clear that they were not wanted.

5. "Fourth Debate; Charleston, Illinois," National Park Service, U.S. Department of the Interior, 2015: https://www.nps.gov/liho/learn/historyculture/debate4.htm.

As far as the South was concerned, such an integrated higher education system would never be accepted, not even after the end of hostilities, not through the period known as Reconstruction from 1865 to 1877, nor in the early years of the Jim Crow laws, to 1890, when the federal government formally accepted the separation of the races. In 1890 Morrill, since 1867 a U.S. senator from Vermont and now eighty years old, offered as legislation a second Morrill Act aimed at the southern states, requiring that each state either demonstrate that race was not a factor in admissions—and now comes the alternative language that would lead to the *Plessy v. Ferguson* Supreme Court "separate but equal" decision of 1896—*or else designate a second state land-grant institution for persons of color.*

It was considered a crime in the South to teach Black Americans to read in 1861. The Civil War, Reconstruction, its failure after 1877, the Second Morrill Land Grant Act, and the Supreme Court decision in *Plessy v. Ferguson* defined the racial issues that would characterize American higher education until the 1960s, in both North and South, in most institutions, public and private.[6]

The Black land-grant institutions authorized in 1890 by the Second Morrill Act, almost totally lacking infrastructure of elementary and secondary school education for Black students, began their work in a hostile

---

6. Private southern institutions followed the same patterns of discrimination right up to the civil rights legislation of the 1960s. See Melissa Kean, *Desegregating Private Higher Education in the South: Duke, Emory, Rice, Tulane, and Vanderbilt* (Baton Rouge: Louisiana State University Press, 2008).

environment. Southern local and state authorities re-fused to provide public high school facilities and only reluctantly contributed to any elementary education, and there was an overwhelming shortage of Black teachers at any level.[7] The federally funded act allowed the states to establish seventeen Black post-secondary segregated colleges and universities. Thelin described their situation: "The seventeen Black institutions were disproportionately neglected with respect to facilities, salaries and staffing. They were ill-equipped to conduct advanced, original research."[8]

Of course, how much of this land, granted for the purpose of education, belonged to those who distributed and sold it cannot be known. The Native American popu-lations of the 1860s were being driven west, further away from their ancestral lands, fighting white encroachment, retreating eventually to reservations—until that land might prove more valuable—and then they were driven off again to even less attractive areas. The institutions established as a result of the 1862 and 1890 legislation offered nothing to the indigenous Americans. Not until 1994 did Congress pass the Equity in Educational Land-Grant Status Act, which created land-grant colleges for Native American populations.

7. "Most obviously, African Americans were radically underrep-resented: in 1937, when roughly 12 million blacks lived in the United States, only 35,000 attended college." Jonathan Zimmerman, *The Am-ateur Hour: A History of College Teaching in America* (Baltimore: Johns Hopkins University Press, 2020), 60.

8. *A History of American Higher Education*, 2nd edition (Baltimore: Johns Hopkins University Press, 2011), 136.

There was also the issue of Christian faith, which would remain an integral part of public higher education into the twentieth century. In the 1890s most of the state public universities held compulsory chapel services and many also required Sunday church attendance. This was a nation of Christian faith, and the Morrill Act institutions reflected it. When it came to matters of higher education, for the most part there was no separation between church and state.[9]

Even with consistent racial issues confronting American higher education from the end of the Civil War to the end of the nineteenth century and into the twentieth, the Morrill Acts created the infrastructure that would eventually lead American public universities to a position of stature then not imaginable. The large, complex state universities—committed to a more practical application of resources for the improvement of agriculture, manufacturing, and what passed for technology at the time—were not yet ready for the basic research role they would eventually play. The public schools were not capable of producing students ready to access a more advanced level of academic activity. Even as the K–12 system in the United States expanded enormously in the second half of the nineteenth century, preparation was uneven, which was reflected in most of our higher education institutions; a disproportionate amount of time and effort was given to remedial courses suitable to a student body unprepared

9. See George M. Marsden, *The Soul of the American University* (New York: Oxford University Press, 1994), 3.

for any semblance of advanced academic activity. As much as American triumphalism soon tried to convince the nation and the world that our universities could compete with those of the Europeans, a more productive focus on research was required. There was no question where the Americans had to look in order to find that unique quality of application and basic research for the benefit of the nation: again, it was Germany.

HIGHER EDUCATION IN THE GILDED AGE: THE COMING OF THE PHILANTHROPISTS

The fact is that until this last century, most Americans had little use for and/or no respect for higher education.

—HAROLD SHAPIRO, former president of Princeton University[10]

Along with William McKinley and Theodore Roosevelt came Daniel Coit Gilman, William Rainey Harper, and David Starr Jordan. All five were presidents and each possessed a new American vision, one that was appropriate for a nation ready to take on the world. Two of them were presidents of the United States and led this country from the recently closed frontier to a new unconquered one across the oceans to Hawaii, the Philippines, Cuba,

10. Ronald G. Ehrenberg, ed., *The American University: National Treasure or Endangered Species?* (Ithaca: Cornell University Press, 1997), 62.

Puerto Rico, and to anywhere that American economic and military power wanted to go. The latter three were the founding presidents of three new private universities, and they, too, were determined to challenge the world: Gilman at Johns Hopkins, founded in 1876; Harper at the University of Chicago, 1890; and Jordan at Stanford, 1891. The energy for these educational enterprises was provided by three enormously wealthy American industrialists— Johns Hopkins, John Rockefeller, and Leland Stanford— who placed the resources of a muscular American capitalism at the disposal of higher education. Few other Americans cared about the future of universities, but they did.

When the German sociologist Max Weber wrote *The Protestant Ethic and the Spirit of Capitalism (Der protestantische Ethik und der Geist des Kapitalismus)* in 1904–5, he had already observed at least twenty-five years of the explosive growth of American industry. That nation had produced a remarkable number of individuals who, in spite of their Protestant piety, accepted that the triumph of science and the free market over faith had catapulted the United States, by the turn of the century, into being a competitive challenger among the world's economic powerhouses. In this American model, the Sermon on the Mount and rapacious, no-holds-barred capitalism could go hand in hand. Business, as it was practiced in the United States after the Civil War, often produced the biggest fortunes for the most ruthless stock manipulators, land speculators, and economic predators focused on crushing all opposition in their quest for monopolistic control over entire industries. These same men were determined that the United States would have a great and competitive university system like the one in Germany, which was most admired by the rest of the world.

The last quarter of the nineteenth century in the United States witnessed events in education that were both regressive and progressive. On the heels of the 1862 Morrill Act and its commitment to public as well as practical education followed the failure of much of the cause over which the Civil War was fought. The four million freed slaves had little access to any education from K–12 and beyond, and by 1877 the entire edifice of Reconstruction and former slave rehabilitation had collapsed, along with the nation's hope for change or racial progress.[11] Most of the millions of acres of grasslands and forests that had been given to the states and territories as grants of land for their public universities through Senator Morrill's legislation had come at the expense of the Native Americans, who had lost faith in a treaty system that had robbed them of any reasonable hope for sustainable land settlements with the United States government. Any white American sympathy was lost after Custer's death at the Battle of the Little Big Horn in June 1876, and Manifest Destiny took over in sweeping the Red Man, along with everyone else of color, from the nation's consciousness. The American journalist and author William Dean Howells characterized progress and the American spirit as the frontier closed in the Far West: "Inequality is

11. It was not a case of simply white versus Black. By 1869 the great transcontinental railroad had been completed, thanks in no small degree to cheap and reliable Chinese labor; this contribution did not prevent the passing in 1882 of the Chinese Exclusion Act barring any further immigration.

as dear to the American heart as liberty itself."[12]Anti-miscegenation laws returned to states in both the South and North. Not until 1967, when the Supreme Court, in *Loving v. Virginia*, struck down the marriage laws in the remaining fourteen racially divided states, was it legal for a white person to marry anyone designated as "colored."

By 1896 the Supreme Court in *Plessy v. Ferguson* had institutionalized separation of the races. The transformation of evolutionary thought begun by Darwin in 1859 had also led to a pseudo-scientific interpretation of race theory that brought eugenics into the biology curriculum of our most prestigious colleges and universities. Inevitably, immigration of "inferior" races became a major political, scientific, and educational issue and in 1894, the Immigration Restriction League was founded at Harvard, with the university's soon-to-be-president Abbot Lowell serving as its vice president. As vice president and later president of the United States, Theodore Roosevelt spoke of the mixing of the Black and white population as "racial suicide," a sentiment repeated by Princeton University's president Woodrow Wilson. There seemed little hope that the American educational system would lead the nation past its racial preoccupation. People from East Asia had virtually no significant presence on American campuses.

American public schools offered few positive expectations. There was enormous growth in attendance in the

12. *Delphi Classics Complete Works of William Dean Howells*, eBook series, https://www.delphiclassics.com/shop/william-dean-howells-2.

final decades of the nineteenth century, yet just six percent of all eligible students graduated from high school in 1900.[13] Even in the elite post-secondary institutions, entering students were woefully unprepared. Abraham Flexner, always a blunt critic of American education at all levels, published data in 1908 on entrance exams at Harvard, Yale, and Princeton showing that two-thirds of entering students failed at least parts of the exams.[14] As the twentieth century began, remedial courses made up significant parts of the first two years of study in most American colleges and universities.

But in the last decades of the nineteenth century, higher education would be redefined by the wealthiest Americans. The unique American idea of philanthropy resulted in the establishment of new private universities with a very specific purpose: to create in the United States institutions of higher learning focused predominantly on research based on the German model. The money came for the most part from enormously successful businessmen who had acquired previously unimaginable wealth. Transportation and communication made all things possible. The oil, steel, and tobacco industries, and the American railroad system as it spread westward to the Pacific, fueled the acquisition of wealth for people named Stanford, Rockefeller, Vanderbilt, Carnegie, Mellon, Duke, and Cornell. As American

13. Richard Rothstein, *The Way We Were? The Myths and Realities of America's Student Achievement* (New York: Century Foundation Press, 1998), 19.

14. *The American College: A Criticism* (New York: Century Company, 1908), 110.

industrial productivity equaled and surpassed that of European nations, these self-made creators of personal wealth turned their attention to the American university.[15] Their intention: to replicate the German quest for basic and advanced research, "hohe Wissenschaft" (high science). There was no place for traditional American undergraduate education, nor for the usual adolescent high jinx or athletic shenanigans. But it didn't quite work out that way.

The first of this new kind of institution came from the fortune of a Baltimore businessman who had made his millions in railroads, banking, and real estate. Johns Hopkins wanted a new type of hospital, medical training, and university. The institution bearing his name, without an undergraduate class anticipated and with an emphasis on science and research, opened its doors in 1876, supported by a $7 million bequest that represented the largest philanthropic gift in American history up to that time.[16] The first president, Daniel Coit Gilman, brought the same energy and sense of competition to the academic enterprise that inspired the businessmen donors. German-trained, he championed research and advanced instruction only for students who were ready for this rigor, which

15. There was no moral test for the naming of an institution. Daniel Drew, a notorious stock manipulator, gave his name and wealth in 1867 to a Methodist seminary in New Jersey that eventually became Drew University.

16. Within a short time, Johns Hopkins was admitting undergraduates, having found that an institution without adequate undergraduate tuition revenue simply did not work as a business model.

eliminated most of the undergraduate population in the United States. As a result, the principal degree from the outset for Johns Hopkins University was the Ph.D.: the German research degree. By the end of the century, faculty from most of the research universities in the United States had earned their degrees from this Baltimore institution.

Gilman constructed the required apparatus for the research university: a university-sponsored press, journals, societies—all incubators for the flow of faculty research and publications. The Johns Hopkins brand was attached to every aspect of this new research enterprise. A year after admitting its first class, Johns Hopkins inaugurated in 1877 its first journal, the *American Journal of Mathematics*, followed quickly by publications for chemistry, biology, physiology, psychology, and philology, all with heavy emphasis on science. Other more venerable Eastern private universities and the newly ambitious public universities in California and Michigan, burdened as they were with hundreds of ill-prepared undergraduates still in need of remedial courses, tried to shift their emphases, but it would take time and the reeducation of faculty who had previously been dedicated exclusively to teaching.

The priority was clear across the culture of this new research community. Education historians soon were choosing sides, and a conflict between teaching and research began that has never really ended. In 1962 Frederick Rudolph characterized it as he saw it: "Publication, indeed, had become a guiding interest of the new academician. Each book, each article, was a notch pegged on the way to promotion . . . It shunted the teacher types off to limbo."[17]

There was disruption and bitterness.[18] By the end of the century, the new research agenda was viewed by many faculties as the platform for the destruction of the American college and traditional university. Harvard's William James deplored "the increasing hold of the Ph.D. Octopus on American life."[19] Historians often could not contain their partisanship in the teaching-versus-research debate. Frederick Rudolph put the blame squarely where he saw it: "The de-emphasis of the teaching role of the American professor was introduced to American higher education at Johns Hopkins." He then launched into an angry characterization of what the Hopkins model had done to American institutions.[20]

There was no stopping the philanthropists and the leaders they selected, infatuated as they were with either faith or German research methods. John Rockefeller, the richest man in the world, wanted a new university for the Baptist Church in Chicago. His search for the right

17. Rudolph, *The American College and University*, 403–5.

18. The most thorough description of this conflict between teaching and research can be found in Zimmerman, *The Amateur Hour*, chapters 1–2, 14–56.

19. *Harvard Monthly* 37 (1903), 1–9. James's cephalopod became the standard image for academics over the next century for research run amok. Princeton's Theodore Ziolkowski suggests that James's octopus had by 1990 morphed into a more aggressive form: "The Ph.D. Squid," *American Scholar*, No. 59 (spring 1990), 178. Jacques Barzun repeated James's warning in 1945, quoted by Ziolkowski: "The octopus has the young teacher in his grip and doesn't let him go."

20. Rudolph, *The American College and University*, 403–9.

man to lead the University of Chicago led him to a young Baptist Hebrew scholar named William Rainey Harper, a dynamo who started college at ten and had earned his Ph.D. at eighteen. In 1891 Rockefeller told Harper to build his university, handing him, at first, an open check-book, and sent him on the road to find a faculty.[21] By the time the University of Chicago opened its doors in 1892, Harper had recruited a first-rate research faculty and, in the process, battered some of his potential competition. Clark University, in Worcester, Massachusetts, established on the German model as one of America's future premier research institutions, never recovered from Harper's weekend raid that took fifteen of the most prominent Clark faculty off to Chicago. Harper brought his competitive zeal to higher education: pay the best and brightest whatever it takes to make them move, and the faculty, wooed by extravagant promises of salary, laboratories, and space, headed for Chicago.[22]

Out west, matters took a similar turn, though under different circumstances. Leland Stanford was as ruthless in the acquisition of his wealth as any of the Eastern financial titans. The building of the great Western railroads

21. President-designate Harper also had to keep a close eye on the religious traditions of his new faculty, since according to the charter of the institution two-thirds of the trustees and the president had to be Baptists. See Veysey, *The Emergence of the American University*, 370.

22. Here is Rudolph's account of the raid on Clark: "The day that Harper arrived in Worcester sixteen faculty and student biologists were engaged in study; twelve of them followed him to Chicago." *The American College and University*, 351. For more on the history of Clark, see "Sigmund Freud Speaks at Clark University (September 7, 1909)", https://www.massmoments.org/moment-details/father-of-psychology -born/submoment/sigmund-freud-speaks-at-clark-university.html.

that joined the nation at Promontory Point in 1869 made Stanford's fortune. His political connections carried his tracks westward on government land, and he became first senator, then governor of California. When his son Leland Jr. died just before his 16th birthday in 1884, he and his wife, Jane, were determined to leave an appropriate memorial. The next year, they made a bequest of $5 million to establish Leland Stanford Jr. University and began building a campus on their Palo Alto farm. They were ready for an opening in the fall of 1891 and went about recruiting a president. They found their man at Indiana University. Forty-year-old David Starr Jordan had been president there for six years, was a well-known professor of zoology, and was a national advocate of protecting the "Nordic race" from mixing with "inferior" peoples. He arrived in Palo Alto in 1891 and set about getting a faculty. Like Chicago's Harper, Jordan was a wunderkind filled with the competitive energy of his founding donor. He headed for Bloomington and Ithaca, New York, where he had gotten his doctorate and began recruiting a faculty. Among his first hires was Edward Alsworth Ross, the founder of American sociology and one of the most outspoken advocates of restrictive immigration, particularly of Chinese workers. Jordan and Ross played prominent roles in passing restrictive immigrations laws for the United States in the 1920s. By necessity, at Stanford there were undergraduates in the first classes as well as remedial courses for these ill-prepared new students. The initial $5 million proved insufficient, and upon Stanford's death in 1893, the university came on harder times. But the widowed Mrs. Jane Stanford threw her considerable fortune into the breach to save her husband's and son's legacy. She became the sole university trustee, with the authority to decide who would stay on the faculty and who would go.

When, a few years later, the Eastern and Midwestern universities presented to Europe the face of American research in higher education, two Western universities, both in California, were considered worthy: the public university, at Berkeley, and Stanford, the private one in Palo Alto.

Legitimacy and acceptance by the Europeans—especially the Germans—was the essential prize for the new American research university. Harvard and Columbia were the first of the established American institutions to accept the new role championed by Chicago and Johns Hopkins in the hunt for research prestige. Presidents Charles Eliot of Harvard, Seth Low of Columbia, Harper, and Gilman asked the University of California's president Benjamin Wheeler to join them in inviting nine other American university presidents to form an association that could impress the Europeans with American academic standards, in the hope of gaining acceptance in the world's academic and business research community. The letter was sent in January 1900 to the other invitees: Catholic University of America, founded by the Vatican as an exclusively graduate institution; Clark University; Cornell University; the University of Michigan; the University of Pennsylvania; Princeton University; Stanford University; the University of Wisconsin; and Yale University—together, eleven private and three public institutions. In a two-day conference in February, these fourteen American institutions drew a line under them that told the rest of the thousands of American colleges and universities: We do research and have shared standards. (For the next century and more, getting into this elite club became the single-minded goal of presidents and boards of trustees across America, as well as the corollary: not getting tossed out because of insufficient research.) The intent of this new organization, the Association of American Universities (AAU), founded the year before the first Nobel Prizes in science were awarded in 1901, was to inform the world that the American universities were ready to take up the international challenge in matters of research, discovery, and invention. More than 80 American learned societies were established in the 1870s, and 121 in the 1880s.[23]

But we were unable to catch the world's academic leaders. The United States remained a nation with intellectual aspirations but not the ultimate accomplishments. The Nobel Prizes in science and other international awards remained, for most of the first four decades of the twentieth century, overwhelmingly in the possession of the Europeans, particularly the Germans. There were ample reasons why the American higher education enterprise continued to play catch-up.

23. See John Higham, *History: Professional Scholarship in America* (Baltimore: Johns Hopkins University Press, 1983), 8.

CHAPTER THREE

Second Best at Best

1900–1940

There were anomalies, distractions, and profound intellectual shortcomings that prevented these American universities from successfully challenging their German rivals.[1] President Harper soon realized that, without undergraduate tuition dollars, the business model would not work. Much as he might have regretted it, the new University of Chicago needed enough undergraduates to make the enterprise financially viable. Rockefeller might have been the richest man in the world, but he never missed an opportunity to hold on to his dollars when the opportunity presented itself. At the end of the day, Harper discovered that the Rockefeller checkbook had a limit, and the young president soon had to face the

---

1. For much of this period, "outsiders" were considered a threat to the academic brotherhood; insularity and homogeneity remained a hallmark of the American faculty right through the first half of the twentieth century. See Sarah Churchwell, *Behold, America: A History of America First and the American Dream* (London: Bloomsbury, 2018).

fact that some of the available undergraduates would not qualify as research-ready. Harper came up with an academic brainstorm: divide the four years of college immediately into two parts. At the first, the usual preparatory remedial courses were offered to students who would be useless in a research lab; at the second, more selective two-year college, better-prepared students could undertake advanced work immediately. Inevitably, this same bookkeeping reality had to be faced at Johns Hopkins; the idea of an all-graduate student research university on the German model had to be adapted to American realities. The ill-prepared undergraduate and advanced graduate research efforts at most of the institutions that called themselves universities were already joined at the hip, even if the parts had very little to do with each other.

It was a marriage of necessity: generally immature undergraduates in a four-year college environment, many working their way through remedial courses for two years, sharing a campus with a research-driven faculty assisted by advanced students seeking the Ph.D. degree. This became the unique problem for the American university model. The quality of the undergraduate teaching and the advanced research might have to be measured by two different standards, since they might involve two different faculties, one that taught undergraduates effectively and one that followed independent basic research. American higher education has been trying to untangle this knot for more than a century since the establishment of the consciously research-driven university.

From the outset, American research universities have been trying to deal with two separate skills within an un-shared context, since not every faculty member possesses the capacity to do both successfully. In the production of research-driven students seeking advanced degrees, there was little priority given to their ability to teach general education to potentially unprepared undergraduates. They were being trained to become independent researchers by assisting experienced older practitioners. The American research university, requiring tuition-paying undergraduates to power the enterprise, created for itself a new dilemma: Do they train teachers or researchers? Do they have the capacity to do both?

THEN THERE WAS FOOTBALL . . .

The current American public mania with intercollegiate sports is historically ingrained in the nation's appetite. Hollywood, always quickly finding the pulse of its audiences, rarely produced a college-themed motion picture in the first half of the twentieth century that did not reflect the football campus culture; even Rockefeller's new university made no effort to avoid it.[2] One of Harper's first Chicago appointments was the already famous football coach Amos Alonzo Stagg, appointed in 1892 with professorial rank and paid more than most of the faculty.

2. See Robin Lester, *Stagg's University: The Rise, Decline, and Fall of Big-Time Football at Chicago* (Urbana: University of Illinois Press, 1995).

Over the next forty years as head coach at the University of Chicago, Stagg—who won two national championships—recruited players, as did all the competitive programs from coast to coast, some of whom could not even marginally satisfy academic standards. A few of these were outright professional "hired guns" who often moved from school to school.

Stagg was one of a group of nationally prominent football coaches associated with these private research universities. Walter Camp was recruited to Stanford along with the first cadre of professors and had his first team in 1892. Fielding Yost, another of the near-professional itinerant football coaches, came for just one season in 1900 before departing for a bigger program at the University of Michigan. He returned to California to play in the inaugural Rose Bowl Game at Pasadena, where his Michigan Wolverines humiliated Stanford's Indians, 49–0. College football in California eventually grew to such a dimension that the Los Angeles Coliseum was begun in 1920 and would grow to an eventual seating capacity of nearly 100,000.

While it remained closest in spirit to the German ideal, even Johns Hopkins University was not immune to American intercollegiate athletic enthusiasm. It fielded its first football team in 1881 and immediately began a rivalry with the Naval Academy that lasted for decades. Although it never reached the football eminence of the University of Chicago or Stanford, the lacrosse program at Johns Hopkins has produced forty-four national titles.

At the highest level of competition among twenty or thirty institutions, intercollegiate football, beginning most prominently around the turn of the twentieth century, had already become a commercial enterprise for the universities and an object of alumni and campus pride, more important than academic standing in the intellectual community. The public demanded appropriate stadiums for the enthusiastic alumni crowds. Harvard completed its large concrete structure in 1903, seating more than 20,000 onlookers. The University of Pennsylvania built Franklin Field in 1895. The University of Chicago football stadium, initially constructed in 1893 on land donated by Marshall Field, eventually would grow in the 1920s to hold 50,000 spectators. Whatever the advocates of "hohe Wissenschaft" and "Lehr- und Lernfreiheit" (freedom to teach and learn) preached in an effort to overtake their betters in Kaiser Wilhelm's Second Reich, football was king on campus in the United States.[3]

EUGENICS AND ACADEMIA

High-grade or border-line deficiency . . . is very, very common among Spanish-Indian and Mexican families of the Southwest and also among negroes. Their dullness seems to be racial, or at least inherent in the family stocks from which they come . . . Children of this group should be segregated into separate classes . . . They cannot

3. Rudolph dedicated chapter 18 in *The American College and University* to "The Rise of Football," 373–91.

master abstractions but they can often be made into efficient workers . . . From a eugenic point of view they constitute a grave problem because of their unusually prolific breeding.

—LEWIS TERMAN, professor of educational psychology, Stanford University, 1916[4]

In 1883 the British scientist and polymath Sir Francis Galton coined the term "eugenics" to describe the results of research he was doing on desirable characteristics in humans that might be heritable, if properly managed. His goal: to improve the human race through inherited intelligence by using statistical methods to study human populations. For a time, the eugenics movement swept the world.

In *The Great Gatsby* (1925), F. Scott Fitzgerald has Tom Buchanan—Yale '15, football star in college, wealthy and privileged—speaking for educated America. Buchanan gives everyone within earshot a taste of his four years of Yale education: "Civilization's going to pieces . . . I've gotten to be a terrible pessimist about things. Have you read *The Rise of the Colored Empires* by this man Goddard? . . . Well, it's a fine book, and everybody ought to read it. The idea is that if we don't look out the white race will be—will be utterly submerged. It's all scientific stuff; it's been proved." Buchanan is referring to Lothrop Stoddard's 1920 bestseller, *The Rising Tide of Color Against White World-Supremacy*. Stoddard had graduated with

4. *The Measurement of Intelligence* (Boston: Houghton Mifflin, 1916), 91–92.

honors from Harvard College in 1905, and received a law degree from Boston University and his doctorate from Harvard in 1914. Buchanan was not reflecting the radical, racist ideas of some fringe element. Indeed, Theodore Roosevelt and Woodrow Wilson were not alone when they spoke openly and wrote freely to condemn the mixing of races. In the first decades of the twentieth century, hundreds of eugenics courses were taught at American colleges and universities, and on some campuses, eugenics biology was the only evolutionary theory presented in the classroom. Harvard, Princeton, Yale, Columbia, Chicago, Cornell, Brown, Wisconsin, Northwestern, Clark, MIT, Johns Hopkins, and Stanford produced most of the leading eugenics-trained advocates for the nation. *Genetics and Eugenics*, by William E. Castle of Harvard, published in 1916, was the teaching tool of choice for most of the biology departments and went through four editions in fifteen years.[5] Science-trained university presidents such as David Starr Jordan (Stanford) and Francis Amasa Walker (MIT) were among the leading spokesmen for eugenics research in the country.[6] Woodrow Wilson, former president of Princeton, spoke for many academic historians and social scientists who shared the eugenicist view of population planning and racial theory.

5. See Julie A. Reuben, *The Making of the Modern University* (Chicago: University of Chicago Press, 1996), 159.

6. Walker, while president of MIT, wrote in the June 1896 issue of the *Atlantic*: "The question to-day is protecting the American rate of wages, the American standard of living, and the quality of American citizenship from degradation through the tumultuous access of vast throngs of ignorant and brutalized peasantry from the countries of eastern and southern Europe."

D. W. Griffith's monumental film *The Birth of a Nation* (1915), a box-office triumph that anticipated the revival of the Ku Klux Klan (KKK) in the American north in the 1920s, was a favorite at the Wilson White House.[7]

Even as the American philanthropists were making their commitment to a new kind of free-ranging research that would drive the engine of progress, the issue of racial contamination, generally in connection with a new wave of immigration from southern and eastern Europe, found a foothold in research universities all over the country. In 1888 the recently established American Economic Association sponsored an essay contest on the theme of "The Evil Effects of Unrestricted Immigration." The winner was the University of Chicago's Edward W. Bemis, Ph.D. Johns Hopkins wrote with scientific dispassion about the essential need of refusing entry to "illiterates" and anyone else "incompatible with the American standard of civilization."[8]

In 1894 three Harvard alumni established the Restrictive Immigration League, stating in its preamble that the organization sought "the exclusion of elements undesirable for citizenship" and "injurious to the national character." Two future presidents of Harvard and MIT would serve on the board of directors. Within two years, so many organizations were advocating restricting

7. See Linda Gordon, *The Second Coming of the KKK: The Ku Klux Klan of the 1920s and the American Political Tradition* (New York: Liveright, 2017).

8. See Aristide R. Zolberg, *A Nation by Design: Immigration Policy in the Fashioning of America* (Cambridge: Harvard University Press, 2006), 199.

immigration by race and ethnicity that an umbrella group was created in 1896, the National Association of Immigration Restriction Leagues.[9]

In the first half of the nineteenth century, Irish immigrants were singled out for a particular kind of nativist racial and religious bigotry. But with a massive immigration from southern and eastern Europe starting in the 1880s, the focus of American eugenicists shifted in the last decades of the nineteenth century primarily to Italians and Jews. Academic research provided scientific evidence of racial distinctions that supported nativist American public opinion, and after World War I the nation marched toward restrictive immigration. The Second International Conference on Eugenics was held in 1923 at the American Museum of Natural History in New York City, where its president, Henry F. Osborn (1857–1935), delivered the keynote address on the conference theme, Eugenics, Genetics, and the Family: "In the U.S. we are slowly waking to the consciousness that education and environment do not fundamentally alter racial values. We are engaged in a serious struggle to maintain our historic republican institutions through barring the entrance of those unfit to share in the duties and responsibilities of our well-founded government."[10]

9. See Daniel Okrent, *The Guarded Gate: Bigotry, Eugenics, and the Law That Kept Two Generations of Jews, Italians, and Other European Immigrants Out of America* (New York: Scribner, 2019).

10. See Steven A. Farber, "U.S. Scientists' Role in the Eugenics Movement (1907–1939): A Contemporary Biologist's Perspective," *Zebrafish*, December 2008, 243–45.

Osborn was one of the nation's most distinguished paleontologists and zoologists. He received his doctorate in 1890 from Princeton, where he remained until Columbia lured him in 1891 with a professorship and an appointment in the New York Museum as curator of vertebrate paleontology. In 1908 he was appointed president of the museum's board of trustees, a position he kept until 1933. From 1909 to 1925 he was president of the New York Zoological Society. His remarks in the opening address to the conference reflect the then-consensus biological wisdom of the American academic community: "In the matter of racial virtues, my opinion is that from biological principles there is little promise in the melting-pot theory. Put three races together (Caucasian, Mongolian, and the Negroid) and you are as likely to unite the vices of all three as the virtues."[11]

Scientific support for these organizations had been primarily provided by respected biologists, psychologists, and statisticians at the great American research universities, both public and private. Johns Hopkins University and its medical school had a significant number of eugenics advocates serving as distinguished professors in leadership positions. The founding dean of the medical school, William H. Welch (1850–1934), was a vocal advocate for eliminating the genetically inferior. He was a founding member of the Board of Science Directors of the Eugenics Record Office at the Cold Spring Harbor

11. Henry F. Osborn, "The Second International Congress of Eugenics Address of Welcome" (1921). The address is available here: https://www.science.org/doi/pdf/10.1126/science.54.1397.311

Laboratory on Long Island, New York, when he wrote: "Why must we start an expensive campaign to keep alive those who, were they intelligent enough, might well curse us for intervening on their behalf? Is not death nature's great blessing to the race? If we have greater power to prevent it than ever before, so much the greater is our responsibility to use that power selectively, for the survival of those of best stock . . ."[12]

The Cold Spring Harbor Laboratory, where the Eugenics Record Office (ERO) was housed when it opened its doors in 1910, was the magnet for academic eugenicists from all over the nation. With generous funding from the Rockefeller, Harriman, and Carnegie fortunes, the ERO became the engine for research, statistics, and eventually instruments of public policy advocating the study of human heredity for the purpose of promoting eugenic legislation that reached both the science lab and the floor of Congress. Improving America's racial stock became the rallying cry for biology departments all over the country. The two scientists most prominently associated with the Cold Spring Harbor lab were Charles B. Davenport (1866–1944) and Harry H. Laughlin (1880–1943). Davenport earned his Ph.D. at Harvard in 1892, and stayed on as a professor of Zoology until he moved to the University of Chicago in 1899. He was elected to the National Academy of Sciences in 1912. Laughlin received his doctorate in biology from Princeton. In 1904 Davenport became the founding director of the Station

12. Melissa Hendricks, "Raymond Pearl's 'Mingled Mess,'" *Johns Hopkins Magazine*, Vol. 58, No. 2 (April 2006).

for Experimental Evolution at Cold Spring Harbor. Six years later, with a gift of eighty additional acres from the Harriman family, the Eugenics Record Office began its operation after Davenport appointed Laughlin as its first director. Together, these two eugenicist administrators provided much of the evidence on race, breeding, and the low mental capacity of non-Anglo-Saxon immigrants that informed the study of biology at American colleges and universities from the turn of the century. Their frequent expert testimony before Congress in the 1920s was written directly into the legislation that closed the doors on southern and eastern Europeans, East and South Asians, and peoples of Arab descent. The restrictive immigration legislation approved overwhelmingly by Congress between 1924 and 1927 reflected the national sentiment: the vast majority of Americans wanted the doors shut.

Whatever scientific evidence was offered on behalf of eugenics research was supported by the most convincing statistical data and newly devised intelligence testing instruments that emerged from Harvard, Princeton, and Stanford. Stanford's Lewis Terman (1877–1956), educated at Clark and Indiana, pioneered in the use of intelligence tests to demonstrate the inferiority of California's Italian, Portuguese, and Mexican school children.[13] Terman's tests were also cited as evidence that two out of five steerage passengers arriving at Ellis Island were feebleminded.[14]

---

13. *Mental and Physical Traits of a Thousand Gifted Children*, Vol. 1 (Palo Alto: Stanford University Press, 1925), 57.

14. Daniel J. Kevles, *In the Name of Eugenics: Genetics and the Uses of Human Heredity* (New York: Alfred A. Knopf: 1985), 82.

Carl Brigham (1890–1943) received all of his degrees from Princeton, remained there as a professor, and became a national leader in the field of psychometrics. He had developed his statistical skills while working on the World War I test program to determine the intelligence of U.S. Army recruits. Brigham published his racial thesis in *A Study of American Intelligence* (1923) and concluded that "the Alpine and Mediterranean races were intellectually inferior to the representatives of the Nordic race."[15] The average intelligence of Black Americans, according to Brigham's research, was approximately that of a ten-year-old.

The godfather of statistical data analysis for the purpose of measuring intelligence was Robert M. Yerkes (1876–1956), who earned a Harvard Ph.D. in comparative psychology in 1902. He accepted a faculty appointment at Harvard and in 1917 became president of the American Psychological Association. It was in this capacity that he undertook an evaluation of the intelligence of the recruits and developed the theories of racial superiority and deficiency that dominated the eugenics movement for the next decades.

Yerkes, Terman, Brigham, Davenport, Laughlin, and their students provided confirmation that in matters of intelligence, race mattered, and that "Nordic" white Americans were far superior in intelligence to other racial groups. All of them provided expert testimony to Congress in the crafting of immigration legislation.[16]

15. (Princeton: Princeton University Press, 1923), 82–83.

16. Of the many studies on the emergence and use of intelligence

In 1936, three years after Hitler came to power in Germany and Nazi racial legislation became the law of the land, Laughlin received an honorary degree from the University of Heidelberg, and Davenport sat on the editorial boards of several German scientific publications. Nazi officials wrote in praise of their work at the Eugenics Record Office.[17]

In the first thirty years after the initial Nobel Prizes in medicine or physiology were awarded in 1901, German scientists won six, along with two dozen in chemistry and physics. Europeans won almost all the rest. In that same period, Americans won none in medicine or physiology. The five Americans who won in chemistry and physics had all trained at some point in pre-Hitler Germany. The one American biologist who was a Nobel winner in 1933, Thomas Hunt Morgan, stated publicly that he had no use for eugenics research.

By the time Hitler's racial policies turned American biologists gradually away from eugenics research in the 1930s, the leaders of the American movement had conveniently grown old. They and their eugenics theory gradually died off in the 1940s, and academic departments at the American research universities quietly buried and forgot them.

---

tests, see Anya Kamenetz, *The Test: Why Our Schools Are Obsessed with Standardized Testing—But You Don't Have to Be* (New York: Public Affairs, 2015), and Nicolas Lemann, *The Big Test: The Secret History of the American Meritocracy* (New York: Farrar, Straus and Giroux, 1999).

17. For the relationship between American and Nazi eugenics, see Stefan Kuehl, *The Nazi Connection: Eugenics, American Racism, and German National Socialism* (New York: Oxford University Press, 1994).

SHUTTING THE DOORS ON CAMPUS

Even before the ascendancy of Hitler's racial science, while many American academic biologists were eager to prove Francis Galton's racial theories, American elite colleges and universities responded to the popular ideas that were leading toward restrictive immigration. What you could restrict from abroad, you could also restrict from within. The flood of Italians and Jews that poured out of Europe and reached America between the 1880s and 1920s caused distress on the campuses of the elite private colleges and universities.

The southern Italians and east European Jews were different from their co-religionists who had arrived earlier in the nineteenth century. The Irish Catholics had suffered in the first half of the century from enormous discrimination in every aspect of American life, but there were almost immediately enough Catholic colleges and universities to provide some access to higher education. Georgetown, Notre Dame, Holy Cross, and Fordham were bastions not only of American Catholicism but of Irish culture and civilization. But no welcome mat was put out by these American Catholic institutions to greet the impoverished Italian peasants who were fleeing their failed farms in the south of Italy. For the most part, the Irish Americans kept their distance. Toward the end of the nineteenth century, they were making it as Americans and left the new Catholic immigrants from Italy to fend for themselves. Grudgingly they made limited room for them in their colleges and universities, but on campus, Catholic American cultural roots were in Ireland.

For eastern European Jews, their reception was no better. About 100,000 German Jews had fled revolution and oppression in mid-nineteenth-century Europe and had made enormous strides in the United States, thanks to assimilation. Along with the much smaller number of Sephardic Jews of Spanish origin, by the end of the century the German-Jewish community was generally Americanized. Many converted, others intermarried, and those who kept their faith found in Reform Judaism a style of worship that suited the American dream. For the most part, they were indistinguishable from their fellow Americans—or at least thought they were. In contrast, the eastern European Jews were followers of Hassidic rabbis who taught a brand of Judaism that was mystical, steeped in traditions of "Yiddishkeit" (Jewishness) and the Yiddish language (called "mama loshen" or the mother's tongue), and separatist in all aspects of daily life. Their followers dressed in long black caftans, wore eighteenth-century styles of clothing, and spoke only Yiddish. The observant men read their holy texts only in Hebrew, the less-educated women in Yiddish. Most German Jews were shocked when they first encountered Jews who looked as if they had just stepped out of a medieval cartoon. Among these former ghetto dwellers were many who rejected traditional Judaism and Torah study in favor of their new God: Karl Marx. They brought their militant political ideology with them across the ocean and engaged in various forms of agitation and union organizing as soon as they settled into their American ghettos.

Many of these younger immigrants, regardless of faith in God or Marx, brought with them a tradition of

Talmudic learning and disputation under which male children were taught that study, analysis of texts, and an argumentative style of give-and-take—pilpul in Hebrew—was the most respected path to wisdom. In Czarist Russia, strict quotas were placed on the few Jewish university applicants who could break away from parental and rabbinic control, but in America things were different. Compulsory education provided opportunity. There was prejudice, but no state devices to prevent studious Jewish kids from pushing themselves forward. By the 1890s Jewish applicants were beginning to cause "a problem" for eastern colleges and universities. The Jewish population of New York City climbed from 80,000 in 1880 to 1,225,000 in 1910.[18] Before World War I, even the most elite colleges had significant numbers of Jewish applications since the colleges at that time took virtually anyone who applied. Application forms were less than a page long. Before they knew it, the campuses were facing large numbers of students very different from those they had come to expect.

At first, the geographically closest institutions were attractive and affordable: by 1918 the City College of New York (CCNY) and Hunter College of the City of

18. See Stephen Steinberg, *The Ethnic Myth: Race, Ethnicity, and Class in America*, updated and expanded edition (Boston: Beacon, 1982), chapter 9, "The 'Jewish Problem' in American Higher Education", 222–52. The issue did not even escape the official Harvard history written by Samuel Eliot Morison: "The first German Jews who came were easily absorbed into the social pattern; but at the turn of the century the bright Russian Jewish lads from the Boston Public Schools began to arrive. There were enough of them in 1906 to form the Menorah Society, and in another fifteen years Harvard had her 'Jewish problem.'" *Three Centuries of Harvard : 1636–1936* (Cambridge: Harvard University Press, 1936), 147.

New York had enrollments that were 80 percent Jewish.[19] But inevitably, the lure of the prestigious American private colleges attracted these intellectually aggressive young men who had been brought up on a diet of Talmudic argument and achievement. What they encountered at Columbia, Harvard, and Yale was a culture of gentility described in 1918 by Thorstein Veblen, an economist and persistent critic of a campus anti-intellectualism that "was pursued to the exclusion of virtually all other values."[20] The "gentleman's C" was the measure of academic achievement for the majority of students. It was considered bad manners to study too hard. In 1904 the Yale yearbook boasted of having "more gentlemen and fewer scholars than any other class in the memory of man."[21]

The aspiring American research universities needed all the academically focused students they could find. Harvard, Yale, Princeton, Columbia, Johns Hopkins, Chicago, Stanford, and the other AAU members were determined

19. The earliest academic study of college quotas is Marcia Graham Synnott, *The Half-Opened Door: Discrimination and Admissions at Harvard, Yale, and Princeton, 1900–1970* (Westport, Conn.: Greenwood, 1979), 16.

20. Veblen was one of the century's earliest and most outspoken critics of American universities and the businessmen who sat on their boards of trustees. He is being rehabilitated by a current generation of academic critics. See *The Higher Learning in American: A Memorandum on the Conduct of Universities by Business Men*, annotated edition, ed. with an introduction and notes by Richard F. Teichgraeber III (Baltimore: Johns Hopkins University Press, 2015).

21. See Jerome Karabel, *The Chosen: The Hidden History of Admission and Exclusion at Harvard, Yale, and Princeton* (Boston: Houghton Mifflin, 2005), 52–58.

to rise to the ranks of the great research universities of Europe. As a result, they started out as meritocracies and looked for the best-prepared undergraduates they could attract, regardless of their origins or manners.

However, at these institutions and other elite colleges that aspired to similar status and prestige, the problem was that meritocracy had little to do with admissions. Between 1906 and 1932, 405 young men applied to Harvard from Groton: 402 were admitted. From the implementation of quotas in the early 1920s until as far along as the early 1950s, admission preferences allowed for what Veysey described as "a homogeneous mass of gentlemen." He also pointed to the "the spectacular rise of athletics" beginning in the 1880s and 1890s right through the first half of the twentieth century, a priority that reflected a national attitude when it came to our colleges and universities. All things considered, college and university admissions found a way to keep the ardent, unwanted, and culturally alien sons of immigrants away from "the fortified bastions of American high culture."[22] It was no different in the professional schools. American medical schools of the 1920s and 1930s had strict—and public—quotas. In 1935 Yale accepted 76 applicants out of 501. Of those, 200 applicants were Jews; 5 were admitted. The Dean gave written instructions to the admissions committee: "Never admit more than five Jews, take only two Italian Catholics, and take no blacks at all."[23]

22. Veysey, *The Emergence of the American University*, 250–276.

23. Gerald N. Burrow, *A History of Yale's School of Medicine* (New Haven: Yale University Press, 2002), 107.

Once the doors were shut, the greater portion of the student body of our most prestigious institutions from the 1930s to the outbreak of World War II was compatible and comfortable, a community of like-minded young people who shared a passion for eating clubs, Greek-letter fraternities with common values, sports, and a healthy resistance to too much intellectual engagement. There are endless memoirs confirming the atmosphere on campus. In 1936 the literary critic Henry Seidel Canby characterized his class, which entered Yale in 1899: "The undergraduate of those days was intellectually a primitive, whose thoughts were busy with athletics, pleasure and social ambition."[24] He concluded that nothing had changed in the intervening thirty years to alter the Yale student body or those at other elite institutions. In 1936 81 percent of the entering class at Princeton had gone to private schools; 63 percent were Episcopalians or Presbyterians, 10 percent were Catholics, and 1.6 percent were Jews.[25]

As the twentieth century began, the racial makeup of the undergraduate population suggested that the Civil War might as well have never happened. What Black students there were at Harvard were not given accommodation in college housing. President Abbot Lowell, who succeeded Charles William Eliot in 1909 and remained president until 1933, thought that students and parents would rise up if he attempted to place Black

24. *Alma Mater: The Gothic Age of the American College* (New York: Farrar & Rinehart), 85.

25. Clifton Hood, *In Pursuit of Privilege: A History of New York City's Upper Class and the Making of a Metropolis* (New York: Columbia University Press, 2016), 330.

undergraduates in traditional dormitory settings. Students of any color were rare. Those who dominated campus life were loyal to alma mater, overwhelmingly white and Protestant, generally deferential, respectful to faculty, and occasionally riotous. Administrations were paternalistic, *in loco parentis*, models of civility. With some noteworthy exceptions, it was a happy and exclusive community of limited intellectual attainment. The German Jews—Stephen Birmingham's *Our Crowd*—who were given a pass to admissions at Harvard, Princeton, and Yale, were grateful and made enormous donations of wealth and art.[26] The Maurice Wertheim collection, donated to Harvard at his death in 1950, instantly made his alma matter one of the largest holders of French Impressionist and post-Impressionist art in the country. The extraordinary growth of the Harvard Fogg Museum collection was made possible by the dedication of Paul J. Sachs, Harvard College Class of 1900, scion of the Goldman Sachs family, who, after retiring from the family business in 1915, while still in his thirties, devoted his life to building the Fogg collection. He was the epitome of German-American Jews' love affair with Harvard, exactly at the time that President Lowell was instituting his quotas on eastern European Jews. Sachs had been asked to sit on the special committee to examine what was considered the unhealthy

26. *Our Crowd: The Great Jewish Families of New York* (New York: Harper & Row, 1967).

number of students of eastern European ethnicity coming to Cambridge.[27]

Putting German Jewish alumni on admissions committees became routine. In the winter of 1931–32, Dartmouth College added select Jewish alumni to its admissions staff to weed out "undesirable" Jewish applicants. The results were reported by President Ernest Martin Hopkins of Dartmouth, which was now admitting "the better types of Jews, rather than . . . the Brooklyn and Flatbush crowd."[28] Columbia University went further. Besides putting German Jews on the admissions committee, they asked these alumni to help craft a special eight-page admissions questionnaire only for New Yorkers, with questions such as, "Did you ever change your name?" A physical examination also became part of the application process for this select group.[29]

In spite of American admiration for the German research paradigm, no more than fifteen American universities were actively engaged in groundbreaking research in 1900, and only Cal Tech joined that group before 1940.[30]

27. See Sally Anne Duncan and Andrew McClellan, *The Art of Curating: Paul J. Sachs and the Museum Course at Harvard* (Los Angeles: Getty Research Institute, 2017). During the Nazi purge of academics, the art history department was one of the few at Harvard that sought out refugee German academics and brought them to America.

28. Quoted in Benjamin Aldes Wurgaft, *Jews at Williams: Inclusion, Exclusion, and Class at a New England Liberal Arts College* (Williamstown: Williams College Press, 2013), 168.

29. Heywood Broun and George Britt, *Christians Only: A Study in Prejudice* (New York: Vanguard, 1931), 72–75.

30. Roger L. Geiger, *The History of American Higher Education: Learning and Culture from the Founding to World War II* (Princeton: Princeton University Press, 2014), 548.

There was also a general embracing on the part of the faculty of the core commonality of American thought and tradition. It was not just biology; English departments reflected the same nativist tradition. Typical of this was the literary movement known as the Southern Agrarianism, led by a group of twelve American writers and academics who wrote a pro-Southern manifesto published as the essay collection *I'll Take My Stand: The Southern and Agrarian Tradition* (1930). Among them were the leading scholars of American New Criticism, the mode of analysis that would soon dominate academic literary scholarship. Southern traditionalists led the way: John Crowe Ransom, Alan Tate, and Robert Penn Warren. One of their great admirers was T. S. Eliot, who in his Page-Barbour Lectures at the University of Virginia in 1933 made clear what this movement was all about: "I think that the chances for the re-establishment of a native culture are perhaps better here than in New England. You are farther away from New York and less invaded by foreign races."[31] He went on to describe why a society with too many Jews is in danger of losing its common identity and to congratulate any American culture that can preserve its racial character.

As the 1930s ended, few observers would have predicted the events of the next two decades that would propel American higher education to world leadership. There had been an explosion in numbers of high school students and graduates, but the standards of American

31. *After Strange Gods: A Primer of Modern Heresy* (London: Faber and Faber, 1934), 16.

secondary school education were suspect. Some selective public-school systems prided themselves on advanced experimental educational research; laboratory schools such as the one at the University of Chicago were magnets for educators seeking a way to improve the overall results from public education. In 1930, America still had 150,000 one-room schoolhouses, and when World War II broke out and the military found itself with millions of draftees, the two biggest problems to confront them were illiteracy and poor oral health. As the 1940s began, the American primary and secondary public-school system was not serving the nation well. But the public did not seem interested.

As for higher education in the first three decades of the twentieth century, faculty from all corners of the American college and university community generally complained about the preparation of entering first-year students. Remedial education continued to consume a great deal of college activity. Intellectualism was suspect. Cornell freshmen held a ceremony each June in which they danced while throwing their books into a flaming fire.[32] Athletics continued to dominate collegiate news across the country. Notre Dame's football coach Knute Rockne may have been the figure most identified with collegiate life in America.[33] Abraham Flexner, a longtime

32. Veysey, *The Emergence of the American University*, 272.

33. See the 1929 report for the Carnegie Foundation for the Advancement of Teaching by Howard J. Savage, *American College Athletics*, in Thelin, *Essential Documents*, 183: "The commercialization of intercollegiate athletic policy in the United States is undeniable."

critic who always had an eye to German superiority, wrote in 1930 (more than forty years after attending Johns Hopkins): "The term 'university' is very loosely used in America. I shall not pause to characterize the absurdities covered by the name . . . [Most] are hotbeds of reaction in politics, industry, and religion. Ambitious in pretension, meagre in performance, doubtful contributors, when they are not actually obstacles, to the culture of the nation."[34]

For anyone seeking the Golden Age of American academic achievement, the period up to and through the 1930s would not be a candidate. Whatever promise had been shown with the success of the private and public research universities championed by the AAU and with occasional international recognition by the Nobel awards, most Americans were indifferent. The national mood was overwhelmingly opposed to any international cooperation. "Americans Only" signs might as well have been added to advertisements for faculty job openings at most U.S. colleges and universities. Restrictive immigration policies were in place; the elite colleges and universities used ethnic and racial quotas for all students and faculty, policies favored by a large majority of the American people. Congressman Martin Dies, a Texas Democrat elected first in 1930, spoke for most Americans in the *National Republic* magazine in 1934, a year after

34. *Universities: American, English, German* (New York: Oxford University Press, 1930), 45.

Hitler's grab of power left many German academics in terror: "We must ignore the tears of sobbing sentimentalists and internationalists, and we must permanently close, lock, and bar the gates of our country to new immigration waves and then throw the keys away."[35]

35. Quoted in Laura Fermi, *Illustrious Immigrants: The Intellectual Migration from Europe, 1930–1941* (Chicago: University of Chicago Press, 1968), 27.

CHAPTER FOUR

National Socialism and the German Universities

1933–1945

"Of all 100 Nobel Prizes in science awarded between 1901, when the awards were founded, and 1932, the year before Hitler came to power, 33 were awarded to Germans or scientists working in Germany. Britain had 18 laureates; the USA produced six."
—*Hitler's Gift: Scientists Who Fled Nazi Germany*[1]

The German academic community rebounded almost immediately from the cataclysmic losses suffered in World War I. Even though the postwar treaties stripped Germany of its patents and industrial secrets—and forbade further alliance between academia and industry of the sort that had created the world's first military-industrial-academic colossus—the Weimar Republic somehow

---

1. Jean Medawar and David Pyke (London: Richard Cohen Books, in Association with the European Jewish Publication Society, 2000), 3.

came to represent another German high point in science and humanities. In atomic physics—with names like Einstein, Planck, von Laue, and Schrödinger in Berlin; Franck and Born in Göttingen; Sommerfeld in Munich; and Heisenberg in Leipzig—the leading young physicists in American research universities felt it was obligatory to spend time in Germany. J. Robert Oppenheimer, who would organize the American effort to build an atomic bomb in the desert of New Mexico in the 1940s, received his Ph.D. at Göttingen under Max Born.

What characterized German academic excellence—and distinguished it from the American model—was the singular public respect that the nation held for its universities. The German people had learned, when Bismarck unified the Second Reich in 1870, about the benefits and progress from German discoveries. It was an authoritarian federal system, but the universities had this magical "akademische Freiheit" (academic freedom) that allowed for independent research and creativity, with a paternalistic government keeping its hands off the researchers, themselves patriotic Germans who were delighted to contribute to the welfare of the nation. The first round of German scientific giants had done their pioneering in the second half of the nineteenth century, when Berlin was the center of the Second Reich; Robert Koch, Rudolf Virchow, and Paul Ehrlich had shown the German people that medical science could make better lives for everyone. Koch discovered the bacterium causing tuberculosis in 1876, Virchow was the founding father of pathology, and Ehrlich pioneered in the chemical treatment of disease. These were national heroes. When Einstein won the Nobel

Prize for physics in 1921, the country celebrated. The German people embraced the idea of intellectual leadership emanating from this great university system, an engine of progress dedicated exclusively to the life of the mind and the welfare of the nation. There was little doubt that Germany had the correct formula to maintain its academic leadership in the world, and the German people revered their scholars and researchers in all fields.

HITLER AND NAZI RACIAL IDEOLOGY

"The great mathematician David Hilbert was asked by a government minister, 'And how is mathematics in Göttingen now that it is free of Jews?' 'Mathematics in Göttingen?' Hilbert repeated. 'There is really none anymore.'"[2]

It is difficult to grasp how quickly Adolf Hitler destroyed the German universities. Ten weeks after coming to power on April 7, 1933, the National Socialist government decreed in the Law for the Restoration of the Professional Civil Service that Jews be dismissed from all university faculties. By 1935 nearly 1,200 Jewish scientists—Jews if one grandparent could be identified by the "Ahnenpass", the hereditary passport that documented official origins—had lost their positions. Only those who could prove their unimpeachable Aryan heredity could teach at German universities. Non-Jewish academics married to Jews were pressured eventually to leave, and many voluntarily did. Some faculty with no

2. *Hitler's Gift*, 29.

Jewish "problems" themselves simply resigned and left Germany. In the Third Reich's first year, 2,600 university positions were vacated. At Göttingen, eleven of the thirty-three physicists and mathematicians were gone; 25 percent of all German physicists resigned or were dismissed, among them past and future Nobel laureates. Many of the faculty were department chairs, heads of their programs, directors of graduate students, and the leading researchers in their fields, not only in Germany but in the world. Albert Einstein was visiting the United States when Hitler came to power; he did not return.

There had been hints of trouble to come. The physics community in Germany had been roiled in the 1920s by charges made against the "new" physics of Einstein and Max Planck by two German Nobel winners, Phillipp Lenard and Johannes Stark. When Hitler came to power, he embraced their doctrine of "Aryan physics" and branded anything associated with Einstein's discoveries and theories of energy as "Jewish physics."[3] Aryan physics became the only acceptable path for physics research at the German universities. Not until Trofim Lysenko's influence on Soviet agricultural research from 1940 until 1965 had a government decree directly impacting scientific investigation so quickly affected an academic discipline. Both also led to destructive consequences for the state.

Wherever possible, the German universities were Aryanized. It was not enough to make the faculties

3. See Philip Ball, *Serving the Reich: The Struggle for the Soul of Physics under Hitler* (Chicago: University of Chicago Press, 2014).

"judenrein" (free of Jews). The academic disciplines themselves had to be "purified." Each defined characteristic of research that could be described as "Jewish" was purged, even in disciplines like mathematics. The process of destroying the world's greatest research enterprise was underway. It would take only a decade and would directly affect the outcome of the world war. Once the critical nuclear scientists had migrated to Great Britain and the United States, the eventual construction of an atomic bomb by the Allies was all but inevitable. There were still German research triumphs. Einstein might have been the symbol of "Jewish physics" for the Nazis, but Newton was all that an ideology founded on "Aryan science" needed. German leadership in rocket research did not depend on nuclear fission. Even as Germany experienced massive round-the-clock bombardment from 1942 to the end of the war, its scientists and engineers were capable of creating havoc in Great Britain and in skies over Europe with the most advanced rockets that the world had ever seen.

As it turned out, for baptized, secular, or observant Jews, Nazism made no distinctions. Many were stunned when they realized that in National Socialist ideology, "Once a Jew, always a Jew." The responses varied. Some, in 1933, embraced the rationale that "This will pass; just sit tight, and sanity will prevail. We are, after all, Germans." Nearly one-third of German Jewry remained in the Nazi state as late as November 9–10, 1938—"Kristallnacht" (the Night of Broken Crystal)—when the German synagogues were burned and destroyed. By then most Jews were trapped, and many who had waited too long perished. But members of the academic community who had been dismissed saw sooner rather than later that their Christian colleagues at the German universities were not about to risk their own careers by protesting. A few outraged gentile academics resigned their appointments; most kept silent. Some, like Stark and Lenard, applauded. And now what?

RESCUE: THE GERMAN ACADEMIC MIGRATION, 1933–1941

The first outstretched hand came from Turkey. By the summer of 1933, a considerable number of German academics had already fled Germany. The country with the closest border and a familiar language was Switzerland, where immediately after the Nazi proclamation, a German emigrant scientist, Philipp Schwartz, created an organization called the Emergency Association of German Science Abroad (*Notgemeinschaft deutscher Wissenschaftler*) in Zurich. His first contact came from the government in Ankara, where Kemal Atatürk's modernization program was reaching into the university system. In the winter of 1933–34, Istanbul University hired thirty dismissed Jewish professors from Germany. Hundreds more would follow. By the end of the war, Schwartz's organization had helped nearly 3,000 German academics find positions all over the world.[4]

---

4. In 2016 a documentary film titled *Haymatloz: Exile in Turkey* told the story of five German-Jewish families who grew up in Turkey in the

In Great Britain, the academic community wasted no time in reaching out to its dismissed German colleagues. Within weeks of the university purges, leaders at Oxford and Cambridge were drawing up plans to help the soon-to-be refugees. In May 1933 Lord Rutherford, president of the Royal Society, Nobel laureate for chemistry in 1908, and Great Britain's outstanding nuclear scientist, announced the creation of the Academic Assistance Council, with himself as president. He organized an appeal for funds that was signed by the forty-two of the most eminent British scientists—forty-one of whom were gentiles—and published in the *Times*.[5] The University of London set up its own network, and by the summer of 1934 fifty-six German academics had found positions in Britain, including thirty-one at Cambridge and seventeen at Oxford. By 1936 the British had provided 1300 positions for refugee scholars.

The entire British academic community seemed to get behind the effort. Three weeks after the Nazi decree and the dismissals, the *Manchester Guardian* published the names of 195 professors who had lost their positions at German universities. Articles and letters appeared in *Nature* appealing for rescue funds. Scholars from other fields also joined in. William Beveridge, director of the London School of Economics from 1919 to 1937, organized the economics profession. He continued his efforts after he

1930s. Also see Arnold Reisman, "German Jewish Intellectuals' Diaspora in Turkey, 1933–1955," *Historian*, Vol. 69, No. 3 (Fall 2007), 450–478.

5. *Hitler's Gift*, 55–130.

was appointed master of University College, Oxford, in 1937. Beveridge approached the Rockefeller Foundation in New York and suggested that it take international leadership for raising funds for the homeless German academicians. But the foundation was unwilling to assume such a visible role.

The Rockefeller Foundation was a puzzle. It continued to fund research in the Nazi state, even building a new Kaiser Wilhelm Institute for Physics in Berlin in 1937. Nevertheless, as soon as the dismissals of faculty had begun in Germany, the foundation set up a special committee to assist American colleges and universities in bringing over the academic refugees. Eventually, the Rockefeller Foundation aided more than 300 Europeans to secure positions in Great Britain and the United States.

THE AMERICAN RESPONSE: RESISTANCE, RELUCTANCE, AND NECESSITY

A few institutions did not miss the opportunity to transform themselves. The Medical School of Tufts College, founded in 1893 in Boston, had been one of those marginal medical schools that Abraham Flexner, in his critical report *Medical Education in the United States and Canada: A Report to the Carnegie Foundation for the Advancement of Teaching* (1910), marked for closing. In fact, he recommended that of the 155 medical schools with such a marginal designation, 124 should shut their doors immediately: the training was poor, the faculty ill-prepared or understaffed, the laboratories inadequate, and the students generally unqualified. But Tufts Medical School gamely soldiered on, adding a two-year college requirement for admission and whatever other improvements it could make with limited resources. The medical school accrediting agency gave the struggling institution at first only "provisional" approval and in the late 1920s suspended its accreditation.

This was the state of things when two Tufts physicians, Joseph Pratt and Samuel Proger, a gentile and a Jew, made a visit to the Rockefeller Foundation in New York in the summer of 1934. They had a proposition: make funds available for transportation, resettlement in America, and basic laboratory facilities, and they would rescue the best German scientists they could find. Now the Rockefeller Foundation agreed. Over the next seven years, thirteen of the finest German scientist-physicians brought their families to settle near Boston. They had to master a new language and a new culture, but their research and teaching resulted in nothing less than a total transfiguration of the struggling medical school. Almost immediately there followed a steady stream of publications (often first translated from their native German), patents, expert (if heavily accented) teaching, and medical diagnoses. Within a year Tufts Medical School received its first full accreditation. No academic institution in the country benefited as much from Hitler's "gift." There were some ironies. Tufts's president John Cousens, who gave initial approval for the overture to the Rockefeller Foundation, had instituted a Jewish quota in undergraduate admissions in 1922.[6]

Other schools saw the opportunity. New York University made transformative strides in the field of mathematics with the recruiting of Richard Courant in 1934 after he was dismissed from his position as director of the Mathematics Institute at the University of Göttingen. Courant's impact eventually led to the creation of the Courant Mathematics and Computing Laboratory and the Courant Institute of Mathematics, co-founded with

---

6. See B. David Stollar, *Out of Nazi Germany in Time, a Gift to American Science: Gerhard Schmidt, Biochemist* (Philadelphia: American Philosophical Society, 2014). Heinrich Brugsch became head of the Arthritis Clinic and the Rehabilitation Department. Alice Ettinger was awarded two gold medals from American radiological societies, was Tufts's first chair of the Department of Radiology, and was adored by generations of students. Joseph Fischmann, professor of urology, was appointed chief of urology at two Boston hospitals. Alfred Hauptmann pioneered in the treatment of epilepsy and muscular dystrophy. Joseph Igersheimer became a leader in surgery for retinal detachment. Heinz Magendantz directed Boston-area cardiac clinics. Martin Nothmann, who in Germany had discovered Sythalin, the first oral antidiabetic agent, served on the Tufts faculty for thirty-nine years and wrote much-cited papers with Pratt and Proger on metabolic disease. Berta Ottenstein, formerly head of the dermatology clinic at Freiburg, published dozens of papers on cell membrane components. Anna Reinauer had a promising career in internal medicine in Germany but never recovered from the trauma of dislocation. Jacob Schloss, gastroenterologist, created new methods for diagnosis of diseases of the stomach. Gerhard Schmidt became a world leader in enzyme research techniques and was elected to the National Academy of Science. Siegfried Thannhauser, who in Germany had been chief of medicine at Freiburg, did groundbreaking research in biochemistry. Richard Wagner, who as a young researcher in Germany had made major discoveries in describing a glycogen storage disease, gave up research completely in America.

Kurt Otto Friedrichs, after Courant was driven out of his position at the Technische Universität Braunschweig. NYU also reinvented itself in the field of art history with the arrival of Erwin Panofsky, who, along with several other refugee scholars, helped propel the Institute of Fine Arts to national and world leadership.

Some colleges and small universities without research agendas—a potential mismatch for German university faculty trained only for research—jumped in. A young art historian named Richard Krautheimer, fired from his post at Marburg, managed to find a position at the University of Louisville in Kentucky and convinced his host that his German associate Justus Bier, another talented art historian preparing for exile, would be a splendid addition to this fledgling art history department. Neither could speak English, but they brought a European luster to the Bluegrass State. Krautheimer soon received an offer from Vassar, the women's college in Poughkeepsie, New York and became the first of the school's three German refugee art historians. He later moved on to Johns Hopkins as a distinguished scholar. Swarthmore and Smith also provided a home for several experimental psychologists.

One of the most improbable pairings landed more than fifty of the refugees at historically Black colleges and universities in the South, where these German outcasts, mostly social scientists and humanists, found themselves in a segregated academic world as racist as the one they had left behind. But for Howard University, Hampton Institute, Tougaloo College, Talladega College, and other all-Black institutions of higher education operating in Jim

Crow America, this was an opportunity not to be missed. Some of the refugees stayed for a few years and moved on; most remained for the rest of their careers in America.[7]

Other American academic organizations, like their British counterparts, jumped in quickly.[8] The Emergency Committee in Aid of Displaced German Scholars, later called the Emergency Committee in Aid of Displaced Foreign Scholars—once again, funded by the Rockefeller Foundation—provided enough money to help several hundred refugee scholars make the transition to the American academic world.[9] Private funds for the refugees were essential, because the majority of the American academic community as well as the alumni were not interested in opening the doors of their alma maters to foreigners. The response from most U.S. private institutions was also less than enthusiastic.[10] By the time the Johnson-Reed Immigration Act became the law of the land in 1924, American public opinion was firmly behind restrictive immigration policies. It had required only

7. Heather Gilligan, "After fleeing the Nazis, many Jewish refugee professors found homes at historically black colleges," Timeline, Feb. 10, 2017, https://timeline.com/jewish-professors-black-colleges-9a61d46 03771.

8. Laurel Leff, *Well Worth Saving* (New Haven: Yale University Press, 2019), provides the most recent research on those universities with active participation, and those with presidents and faculties who were reluctant or wanted no part of the immigrant scholars.

9. The archive can be found in the New York Public Library, http://archives.nypl.org/mss/922.

10. Wayne J. Urban and Marybeth Smith, "Much Ado About Something? James Bryant Conant, Harvard University, and Nazi Germany in the 1930s," *Paedagogica Historica: International Journal of the History of Education* 51, Nos. 1–2 (2015), 152–65.

two years for the Harvard-inspired movement to become nationwide with the establishment of the National Association of Immigration Restriction Leagues in 1896. Even as cheap labor poured in through the recently opened Ellis Island (1892), efforts had already begun in Washington to legislate change in immigration law. Bombings, race riots, and labor agitation pushed public opinion over the next two decades toward shutting the doors on immigrants. Congressional hearings, the arrests and trial of the radical anarchists Sacco and Vanzetti, and more bombings led to the anti-immigration laws and the establishment of college quotas based on race and ethnicity. By the mid-1920s and 1930s, the nation was overwhelmingly in favor of these policies. With this attitude firmly in place, there was little enthusiasm for bringing any foreigners into our academic institutions.

When Hitler's decrees overturned the lives of hundreds of German academics, Edward R. Murrow, then a senior staff member with the Emergency Committee in Aid of Displaced Foreign Scholars, wrote of the "general indifference" of the American academic community to the plight of their German and later European colleagues. Murrow said that most Americans considered what was happening in Germany as strictly "a Jewish problem." In the 1930s, anti-Semitism was imbedded in the marrow of American public opinion.[11] Henry Ford's virulent newspaper the *Dearborn Independent*, radio talks by the Catholic priest Father Charles Coughlin that reached more than thirty million weekly listeners, and the public

11. *Hitler's Gift*, 62.

spectacles of Ku Klux Klan parades through the streets of the nation's capital authentically reflected the national attitude toward foreigners, and especially Jews.[12]

It is not surprising that the doors of American colleges and universities were not quickly thrown open to these German outcasts in 1933. Bernard Bailyn and Donald Fleming opened their historical study of the intellectual migration by noting: "The migration was not a mass movement. Of the millions of Europeans uprooted by the Fascist regimes, only a small proportion was able to reach safe refuge abroad, and of those only a trickle managed to settle in the United States." They chronicled the resistance of the American academic establishment, no matter how distinguished these exiles were.[13] Most of them were Jews, which only added to the resistance on the part of an overwhelmingly Protestant-entrenched academic culture. Bailyn and Fleming: "American scholars and European visitors were aware of anti-Semitic attitudes and un-written policies with the science departments of many American universities. They recall that even under ordinary circumstances in the 1920s and early 1930s it was often especially difficult to find faculty positions for well qualified Jewish graduates."[14]

However, no other nation could offer the scale of possibilities that the United States had available in sheer

12. See James Q. Whitman, *Hitler's American Model: The United States and the Making of Nazi Race Law* (Princeton: Princeton University Press, 2017), 34.

13. *The Intellectual Migration: Europe and America, 1930–1960* (Cambridge: Harvard University Press, 1969), 3.

14. Ibid., 216.

number of institutions. With thousands of colleges and universities both public and private, and despite the financial stress caused by the national Depression, American resources were greater than those of the rest of the free world combined.

The American government offered no assistance; quotas on German immigration were not increased. In 1938 more than 300,000 Germans—mostly Jews who had been stripped of their citizenship—had applied for visas and entry permits; about 20,000 were approved. The language of the law denied entry to anyone "who might become a public charge." For the German Jews who had been stripped of all possessions, this constituted a guaranteed rejection, unless they could find enough aid from the few refugee organizations in America trying to get them out.[15] What aid would come was made available through private foundations and faculty efforts at some institutions. With public opinion overwhelmingly opposed to admitting more refugees, the State Department refused to alter the German quota or the restrictions.[16]

Along with the essential mathematicians, the field of nuclear physics shifted its center of gravity from Germany

15. *Constitutional Rights Foundation*, "Educating about Immigration: History Lesson 5: U.S. Immigration Policy and the Holocaust," http:// crfimmigrationed.org/lessons-for-teachers/144-hl5.

16. Even after the much-publicized burning of the German synagogues on November 9–10, 1938, a poll suggesting that 10,000 additional German Jewish children be admitted outside of the quota showed 60 percent of Americans opposed. A year later, when the SS *St. Louis* was turned back from an American port with 1000 German refugees, public opinion had not changed. See Okrent, *The Guarded Gate*, 373–74.

to America and Great Britain. Einstein, although past his most creative period, nonetheless became the light that attracted the greatest minds in the world to American academic homes: Hans Bethe, Felix Bloch, Niels Bohr, Hans Courant, James Franck, Rudolph Peierls, Otto Frisch, and Lilli Hornig, and the Hungarians Edward Teller, Eugene Wigner, John von Neumann, and Leo Szilard all would eventually spend time working on the building of an atomic bomb in the New Mexico desert, and these represented only a fraction of European scientists who fled the Nazis. The letter sent to President Roosevelt in August 1939 was a collaboration between Szilard and Wigner, who drafted it for Einstein's signature, informing President Roosevelt of recent discoveries that might make possible "extremely powerful bombs of a new type."[17]

Mussolini's Fascism didn't turn anti-Semitic until 1938, when he capitulated to Hitler and proclaimed *The Manifesto of Race*, which then endangered Enrico Fermi's Jewish wife, Laura, and his children. Fermi left, ostensibly to get his Nobel Prize in Stockholm. After receiving his award, he left immediately for the United States. His creation of the world's first nuclear reactor, the Chicago-Pile 1, in December 1942, earned him the title "architect of the nuclear age and atomic bomb" and made possible the creation of the atom bomb at Los Alamos, New Mexico, three years later.

17. Albert Einstein to President Roosevelt, August 2, 1939. See: https://www.osti.gov/opennet/manhattan-project-history/Events/1939 -1942/einstein_letter.htm.

Fermi had never thought of his children as Jews. They were assimilated, thoroughly Italian, and secular. For the German Jews who found themselves in the net of Nazism, they initially believed that their identification as fully assimilated Germans, even baptized Christians, would provide all the proof they would need. It didn't. Fermi also had some difficulties with American immigration. Italians had been placed in the same undesirable category as eastern Europeans in the 1920s; Al Capone's criminal conviction and the Sacco and Vanzetti events were still fresh in the minds of Americans. The KKK particularly singled out Catholics and Jews in their 1920s and 1930s reincarnation. Fortunately, when Fermi's visa was held up, some American government officials intervened.[18]

The United States produced some remarkable individuals who threw themselves into the struggle to save European intellectuals and academics. The American journalist Varian Fry had visited Berlin in 1935 and became an eyewitness to Nazi policies. From then on, he dedicated himself to writing about Hitler's Germany, and after the invasion of France in 1940 he joined the Emergency Rescue Committee and headed to Marseille, where during the Vichy collaborationist period he smuggled thousands of desperate refugees across the mountains into Spain and then Portugal. A year later the State Department acted on complaints from Vichy and forced his return to the United States.[19]

18. Laura Fermi, *Illustrious Immigrants*, 26–27.

19. See Andy Marino, *A Quiet American: The Secret War of Varian Fry* (New York: St. Martin's, 1999).

At individual colleges and universities, American colleagues acted. The Princeton faculty donated 5 percent of their salaries in 1933 to the Academic Assistance Council in England. But campuses did not universally welcome Hitler's academic outcast. Right up to and beyond Pearl Harbor, polls showed that over 80 percent of the American population were opposed to raising quotas for Jewish refugees, and in 1935 the British Academic Assistance Council was told by an American envoy that "there was no more room for academic refugees."[20]

The United States entry into World War II helped quiet somewhat the racial prejudices and general nativism that could be found in most academic communities in America. Reluctantly, even English departments at Columbia, Harvard, Princeton, Yale, and other elite institutions would seek out a promising Jewish scholar, who, if he fit—had the right accent and manners—could gain tenure in the gentile-dominated halls of these universities.[21] But not everywhere. For example, at my own institution, Tufts University, the public policy of the English Department well into the postwar years was to hire exclusively Protestant male candidates from the Harvard graduate program.

20. *Hitler's Gift*, 135.

21. See two books by Susanne Klingenstein, *Jews in the American Academy, 1900–1940: The Dynamics of Intellectual Assimilation* (New Haven: Yale University Press, 1991), and *Enlarging America: The Cultural Work of Jewish Literary Scholars, 1930–1990* (Syracuse: Syracuse University Press, 1998).

After December 7, 1941, scientific and military-related research trumped any bigotry, at least in the research laboratories. The academic conscience was also stirred somewhat by Hitler's excesses. Even before he began the systematic killing of Jews and Roma of Europe, Nazi eugenics policy for the purification of the Germanic race led to the elimination of individuals affected by Down Syndrome and anyone characterized generally as "mentally or genetically defective" according to the racial laws of Nazi Germany. During the 1930s, even Germans were protesting the indiscriminate killing of inmates in asylums and hospitals.[22] In the United States, this eugenically based German public policy caused enough outrage to bring discredit to the widely accepted eugenics movement that then dominated American biology. Abruptly, eugenics research in America lost credibility, and, more importantly, funding. Eugenics in America was quietly discarded.

Very few academic centers in the United States were prepared to tackle war-related research. MIT made important breakthroughs in crypto-analysis—the earliest research leading to codebreaking—microwave technology, and research on radar. The Johns Hopkins Applied Physics Lab worked on proximity fuses along with other critical instrumentations, and the enormous Manhattan Project to build the atomic bomb brought faculty from their campuses to government-built projects in

22. See John Cornwell, *Hitler's Scientists: Science, War, and the Devil's Pact* (New York: Viking Penguin, 2003), 348ff.

Oak Ridge, Tennessee; Hanford, Washington; and Los Alamos, New Mexico. But, for the most part, American higher education was reluctant to grab the golden ring that Hitler had handed the United States. The generation of senior faculty who dominated intellectual life, such as it was in American colleges and universities, had with rare exceptions a vision of American achievement that was based on narrow racial and ethnic beliefs. By the end of World War II, there had been two decades of restrictive immigration and ethnic quotas in college admissions, both undergraduate and graduate. Some argued that, without the immigrant scientists, we would not have won the war. However, as the conflict came to an end, there had to be someone out of the ordinary who could envision the possibilities for American higher education.

Our homegrown academic products showed streaks of genius. Ernest Lawrence, a graduate of the University of South Dakota, University of Minnesota, and Yale, in 1930 became the youngest full professor at the University of California at Berkeley and won the Nobel Prize for physics in 1939 for inventing the cyclotron. Arthur Compton attended the tiny College of Wooster in Ohio, got his Ph.D. from Princeton in physics, and won his Nobel in physics in 1927. Each played a critical role in the building of the atom bomb. But when it came to national adulation, we preferred our native geniuses without academic credentials: Thomas Edison, Henry Ford, and the Wright brothers.

America's position among the world's industrial nations had not attained what the Gilded Age philanthropists had hoped for—not surprising if one considers the state of K–12 education, restrictive immigration laws, general indifference to intellectual accomplishment among Americans, ethnic quotas on who could gain admittance to elite post-secondary institutions, racial problems reflected in the Jim Crow South, and discrimination against people of color in virtually every part of the nation. On the verge of America's forced end to its isolationism, as the world plunged toward conflict in the fourth decade of the twentieth century, the United States at the outset of hostilities seemed in no position to assume international leadership in anything, let alone higher education. Gunnar Myrdal's *An American Dilemma: The Negro Problem and American Democracy* (1944), sponsored by the Carnegie Corporation of New York, laid out the reasons why millions of nonwhite American citizens could not participate fully in the American experience. He started his research in 1938 and in nearly 1500 pages chronicled the history of what he called "the white man's problem" that led to the failure of American education to cure racism. In the pre–World War II South, there were 200 counties with large Black populations with no high schools where they could be admitted.[23] The Chinese Exclusionary Act of 1882, America's first law to prevent a specific ethnic group from immigrating to the United States, was not repealed until 1943. Before that students of Chinese

23. Robert M. Hutchins, *Some Observations on American Education* (Cambridge: Cambridge University Press, 1956), 21. Former president of the University of Chicago, Hutchins wrote this book primarily for a British public. Like Myrdal, he believed that the United States could not advance until the nation had confronted its racial issues.

extraction were virtually excluded from American college and university campuses. Whatever modest presence Japanese Americans had in higher education disappeared with the forced relocation of over 100,000 people of Japanese ancestry starting in February 1942. Over 60 percent of those interned were American citizens. With post-secondary opportunities for any people of color limited, American academia relied heavily on an overwhelmingly white population of young people who, until that point as the nation prepared for war, had not demonstrated a capacity to take on the world in intellectual—particularly scientific—accomplishment.

With the coming of American involvement in World War II, many in the world of education were frankly worried, even if the public didn't seem to care. In 1940 it was estimated that 14 percent of all potential draftees were illiterate.[24] Fewer than 40 percent of the sixteen million Americans who eventually served in the armed forces had graduated from high school.[25] It made no difference if they came from the North or South; illiteracy rates in New York State and Pennsylvania were equally as high. Allan Nevins's research on the dismal state of geographic and historical literacy among entering first-year students led to a series of *New York Times* articles. More than a year after Pearl Harbor—on April 4, 1943—the *New York*

24. Christopher Loss, *Between Citizens and State: The Politics of American Higher Education in the 20th Century* (Princeton: Princeton University Press, 2011), 102.

25. Paul Tough, *The Years That Matter Most: How College Makes or Breaks Us* (Boston: Houghton Mifflin, 2019), 313.

Times greeted readers with a bold front-page headline: "Ignorance of U.S. History Shown by College Freshmen: Survey of 7,000 Students in 36 Institutions Disclosed Vast Fund of Misinformation on Many Basic Facts." The reporter, Ben Fine, soon to be the paper's education editor, had written an earlier front-page article on June 21, 1942, soon after Nevins's *Times Magazine* piece and using Nevins's data, with the headline "U.S. History Study Is Not Required in 82% of Colleges." Nevins and Fine were concerned; the rest of the nation didn't get particularly excited. Fine, who later became dean of the School of Education at Yeshiva University, continued his editorializing headline crusade: American youth embarked upon an unprecedented period of global involvement, fighting for American principles on every continent. How could they be so ignorant of their American heritage, not to mention a woeful unfamiliarity with a map of the world?

World War II changed everything.

CHAPTER FIVE

Taking Us to the Top
of the Mountain

A Man Named Bush

"Of the men whose death in the summer of 1940 would
have been the greatest calamity for America, the President is first, and Dr. Bush would be second or third."

—ALFRED LOOMIS, deputy director,
  National Defense Research Committee[1]

His first name was pronounced "Van-EE-ver" and very
few people got it right. He is arguably the least-known
among the most important Americans in twentieth-
century history. Even though his name is unrecognizable to the vast majority of educated Americans, he is
responsible in large degree for the enormous research
achievements of American universities, as well as the
success of our higher education establishment in general

---

1. G. Pascal Zachary, *Endless Frontier: Vannevar Bush, Engineer of
the American Century* (New York: The Free Press, 1997), 106. See also
Robert E. Sherwood, *Roosevelt and Hopkins: An Intimate History* (Harper
& Brothers: New York, 1948), 153–56.

in the twentieth century, and the continued worldwide leadership of American universities going into the third decade of the twenty-first century. The extraordinary scientific accomplishments of our academic and industrial communities over the decades since the end of World War II can be traced back in large degree to one man: Vannevar Bush.[2]

He was an authentic New England product, born in 1890 in Everett, Massachusetts, the only son of a local Universalist minister Perry Bush, who, like most the of his fellow denominationalists, attended Tufts College in Medford—the first college and seminary in America, established in 1852 by this most tolerant group of Protestants. He was named after his father's college friend, John Van Nevar, who also attended Tufts College. The apple was not intended to roll far from the tree. By the time it stopped rolling, the Allies had won World War II and civilization was well on its way to scientific and technological achievement in cognitive learning and information theory, the architects of which, among others, were Vannevar Bush, Norbert Wiener, John von Neumann, Claude Shannon, and Alan Turing. But only Bush possessed the organizational genius and temperament to bring the government into the process of scientific creativity and midwife the birth of the Information Age that would eventually take the world to its current stage,

2. Only Wikipedia reflects his role in the evolution of the American university: Clark Kerr has five pages in his entry, Nicolas Murray Butler seven, Robert Maynard Hutchins eight, Harvard's Abbott Lawrence Lowell fifteen, and Vannevar Bush sixteen.

as it approaches the mid-twenty-first century and a future with artificial intelligence we can scarcely imagine.

Bush found himself in a position at the right moment in history, with the instruments of governmental power in his hands—thanks to a president who had complete faith in him—to make decisions and influence policy, even when he failed to convince his numerous opponents, decisions that would affect the course of American higher education for the next century. This quintessential Yankee, a politically conservative Republican—at times prickly, elitist, even arrogant—preferred people very much like himself as his closest confidants. He didn't like it when the Supreme Court struck down the "separate but equal" doctrine in 1954; up to that time, Bush might not have ever met a Black scientist and didn't believe that giving equal opportunity to Black Americans would add to the national pool of talent.[3] Yet he possessed that remarkable American inventiveness characteristic of Edison and other intuitive thinkers: a creative mind, a technological vision, and an entrepreneurial spirit, joined with an extraordinary knack for bringing together people—scientists and engineers—for the purpose of unleashing scientific and technological innovation in the service of his country. It was unlikely that he had ever met anyone like J. Robert Oppenheimer or Leo Szilard, but his faith and admiration for these physicists, so different in background and temperament, provided the support that made Los Alamos and the building of

3. Zachary, *Endless Frontier*, 369.

the atomic bomb possible.[4] When the government re-
voked Oppenheimer's security clearance in 1953, Bush
was one of the first to come forward in Oppenheimer's
defense. He admired Charles Lindbergh and called him
a friend, but Bush's grounded intellectual integrity led
him to dismiss out-of-hand Lindbergh's belief that German technological and scientific leadership was invin-
cible. It was Bush's organizational agility that empow-
ered the near-anarchic scientists at Los Alamos and
allowed Oppenheimer and General Leslie Groves to
build the Manhattan Project on an unprecedented scale.
It was Bush who held at a critical moment even before
Pearl Harbor all the strings that would give the United
States the ultimate victory in World War II, after which
he became the godfather of post-war Big Science and the
enabler of the American universities' race to the top. Of
all the government functionaries surrounding President
Roosevelt in the war years, only Bush had total faith in
the need for independence for the American scientific
community: just give them the money and get out of
the way. It is difficult to believe that someone coming
from the frugal tradition of New England Puritan Prot-
estantism had the capacity for fiscal risk-taking that lay

4. His sister Edith Bush, while dean at Tufts College/Jackson College for Women, would routinely arrange for the four Jewish first-year
students at Jackson, who were admitted under the Tufts quota, to room
with each other. After a year of friend-making, some would occasionally try to room with a gentile, only to be told by Dean Bush, "You'll
be happier with your own kind." See Sol Gittleman, *An Entrepreneurial
University: The Transformation of Tufts, 1976–2002* (Hanover, N.H.: University Press of New England), 147.

at the heart of Bush's belief that the American scientist possessed unlimited inventiveness, and once unleashed, would produce generations of national treasure.[5]

Even before the beginning of America's involvement in the war, Bush was preparing himself for his ultimate role. He graduated from Tufts College in 1913 with both a B.S. and M.S. in electrical engineering, and three years later received his doctorate in engineering jointly from Harvard and MIT. He started immediately inventing a variety of thermostatic switches, radio tubes, and electronic instruments, partnered and collaborated to form businesses, and in 1922 rose to a position as director of a company that eventually would become Raytheon Corporation. By 1927 the now-wealthy entrepreneur—not yet forty—turned his mind to information acquisition and invented an instrument he called "a differential analyzer"; the evolution of computing had just taken a large step forward.[6] In 1932 he was appointed dean of the School of Engineering at MIT, and the additional title of vice president was created for him, allowing Bush to range all over the institute to seek out collaborative scientists for large-scale research. It was only a matter of time before

5. See David A. Hollinger, *Science, Jews, and Secular Culture: Studies in Mid-Twentieth-Century American Intellectual History* (Princeton: Princeton University Press, 1996).

6. This was the beginning of Bush's vision of what eventually became the Internet. In 1945 he wrote in the July issue of the *Atlantic*: "Consider a future device in which an individual stores all his books, records, and communications, and which is mechanized so that it may be consulted with exceeding speed and flexibility. It is an enlarged intimate supplement to his memory."

the national scientific community saw what he could accomplish, and in 1938 he was made president of the Carnegie Institution for Science in Washington, D.C. Bush now had oversight of eight major research laboratories, and from this influential perch he could create science policy right under the nose of the disinterested federal government.

He was not afraid to take blunt direct action when his judgment told him that something was wrong. The Carnegie Foundation had been a major source of funds for the eugenics movement, particularly the Eugenics Record Office under Harry H. Laughlin. Bush immediately cut off funding, changed the name to the Genetics Record Office, and told Laughlin that his tenure was over. He also cut back funding on projects related to the humanities and social sciences, for which he had little use.

Now every scientific committee wanted him. In 1938 Bush was also appointed to the National Advisory Committee for Aeronautics, soon becoming vice-chairman and then acting chairman. The isolationist American people were not taking notice, but Bush was preparing the nation for the war he saw coming. With the support of the peacetime chief of the Army Air Corps, Major General Henry ("Hap") Arnold, who would become one of the operational architects of the Allied victory, Acting Chairman Bush proposed a massive upgrade of aeronautical research. After maneuvering through congressional appropriation committees for a year, he secured $11 million—about $210 million in current dollars—for a California-based research center, selected by Bush because of the availability nearby of academic scientists and industrial aviation researchers.[7]

While Hitler was rampaging across Europe in June 1940, Bush, who had enough of Congress for the moment, figured out a way to arrange a private White House meeting with President Roosevelt, with only Harry Hopkins, FDR's trusted advisor, in the room. Bush gave the President a one-page memo proposing a National Defense Research Committee (NDRC), "with funds . . . for financing research in laboratories of educational and scientific institutions or industry."[8] In just fifteen minutes, Roosevelt initialed his approval. The American academic community was about to get its first enormous infusion of federal dollars.

But even this funding satisfied neither FDR nor Bush, who was quickly becoming the President's primary science advisor. After Bush met in August 1940 with a British scientific delegation led by Henry Tizard, he found funding for a laboratory which he insisted be located at MIT to work on British advances in radar technology. Called the Radiation Lab, it did as much to defeat the Nazi forces in Europe as the atom bomb did to end the war in the Pacific. The necessary permanent government funding of these huge projects was accomplished in June 1940 when the president signed an executive order creating the

7. The National Advisory Committee for Aeronautics—NACA—was the incubator under Bush's leadership for its successor organization, NASA.

8. Zachary, *Endless Frontier*, 112.

Office of Scientific Research and Development (OSRD), with Bush as director and a congressional mandate for funding. Bush, who was planning to launch an all-out crusade against disease that would transform American biomedical institutions, insisted on one additional program: basic medical research. His eventual instruments would be the National Institutes of Health (NIH). Eighteen months before Pearl Harbor, Bush wanted medical research included in the war effort that he saw as inevitable. While most of the nation cheered Notre Dame football for "winning one for the Gipper," this tough-minded Massachusetts engineer was laying the groundwork for the greatest leap forward in the history of American higher education and the dominance of the American research university for generations to come.

Nothing demonstrated Bush's capacity to manage enormous complexity and get things done, even during a period of national isolationism, like the preparation for the building of the atom bomb. When two German physicists, Otto Hahn and Fritz Strassmann, announced the discovery of uranium fission in the German publication *Die Naturwissenschaften* on January 6, 1939, immigrant scientists already in the United States were terrified that the Nazis might get a uranium-based nuclear weapon. An earlier Hahn collaborator, the German Jewish scientist Lise Meitner, already in exile, identified the Hahn-Strassmann uranium reaction as nuclear fission. Six months later, Einstein signed a letter dated August 2, 1939, written by two exiled Jewish physicists in America,

Leo Szilard and Eugene Wigner, to President Roosevelt, warning him of the possible building of an atom bomb by the Germans and urging him to action. Once Roosevelt grasped the danger and the need to get ahead of the Germans a few months later, he set up an Advisory Committee on Uranium. But the government bureaucracy bogged down, and research and development on fissionable material and progress on building an atomic military weapon went nowhere. When Bush was put in charge of overall military research as head of the OSRD in June 1941, he immediately placed the uranium committee under his direct supervision and, with Roosevelt's approval, ordered a crash program to build an atom bomb. It was secretly called the Manhattan Project, since one of the earliest labs was located in an abandoned Nash automobile plant on Manhattan Island. He cut through military bureaucratic competition, put the Army in charge, approved General Groves as overall leader, and signed off on Oppenheimer's scientific team in Los Alamos, New Mexico. Bush saw to it that the enormous amount of funding would be available and that the scientists would be given as much free rein as possible. Bush had direct supervision of these three monster projects in New Mexico; Hanford, Washington; and Oak Ridge, Tennessee, spending billions, building synergies between American research universities and industry, and preparing for a future of American higher education that previously had been inconceivable. When the first test of an atomic weapon took place at the Trinity site in New Mexico on July 16, 1945, hundreds of European scientists, besides

Bush, had their fingerprints on the project. Most of them were either already or soon-to-become American citizens, and most would find their way to academic positions or to industry. Here was one of the first building blocks of the edifice on which American university research hegemony would be built after World War II.

No wonder that just over a year earlier Bush appeared on the cover of *Time* on April 3, 1944, described as "The General of Physics."

PREPARING FOR PEACE

Many insiders suspected in 1944 that President Roosevelt was dying. Though FDR must have realized that he might not complete his term in office, he showed little interest in the selection of a vice president at the Democratic convention. The final year of the war drew off what little strength he had left. A cardiologist who was brought in was shocked at the degree of deterioration in the president's condition. His strength was draining away, and his attention to anything other than the immediate victory over the Axis barely showed.

There was no doubt who wrote a detailed and meticulously clear two-page letter from FDR to Bush dated November 17, 1944, requesting a peacetime plan for the continuation of the research efforts led by the OSRD; it was the man from whom FDR was seeking recommendations—Bush himself—and the letter reflected Bush's faith in the American academic and industrial communities. In effect, Bush was instructing FDR about the future, emphasizing four points: (1) How fast can we tell the world of the enormous strides we have made scientifically during the war? (2) How quickly can we direct resources for an all-out "war of science against disease?" (Here Bush was preparing for his anticipated expansion of biomedical research that would transform academic medicine in the United States forever.) (3) How can the federal government assure that both public and private organizations are engaged in this research effort? (4) To quote directly from the letter: "Can an effective program be proposed for discovering and developing scientific talent in American youth so that the continuing future of scientific research in this country may be assured on a level comparable to what has been done during the war?" Four months earlier, the Servicemen's Readjustment Act of 1944, commonly known as the G.I. Bill of Rights, was signed into law. In this fourth and final point of his letter "from FDR" to himself, Bush was preparing the nation for nothing short of an academic revolution that would make postwar American higher education virtually unrecognizable from pre-war.[9] Like a Mozart of higher

9. "The transformation of the postwar American university was so extensive that it resulted in a wholly new institution, qualitatively different from that of the first half of the century. The expansion of higher education after 1945 was transformative, both at the level of individual institutions and the national system as a whole." Wilson Smith and Thomas Bender, eds., *American Higher Education Transformed, 1940–2005: Documenting the National Discourse* (Baltimore: Johns Hopkins University Press, 2008), 1.

education, Bush could envision the entire completed score in his imagination and was taking steps for the nation to share this vision.

Before the ghostwriter could complete the reply to his own mandate, the putative author of the letter was dead: FDR died on April 12, 1945. Bush waited a respectful three months before sending President Harry Truman a cover letter, summary, and the document of over two hundred pages, titled "Science: The Endless Frontier." "It is clear from President Roosevelt's letter that in speaking of science he had in mind the natural sciences, including biology and medicine, and I have so interpreted his questions," Bush wrote to the new president. "Progress in other fields, such as the social sciences and the humanities, is likewise important, but the program for science presented in my report warrants immediate attention." Here was Bush, speaking as if instructed by the late beloved American president, setting the course for American academic hegemony for far into the future: American science would lead the world.

He wanted the new President Truman to have the same faith in his judgment that FDR had shown, and to continue the postwar programs in science and research that Roosevelt had endorsed. "The pioneer spirit is still vigorous within the nation. Science offers a largely unexplored hinterland for the pioneer who has the tools for his task. The rewards of such exploration both for the Nation and the individual are great. Scientific progress is one essential key to our security as a nation, to our better health, to more jobs, to a higher standard of living, and to our cultural progress."[10]

Bush, certain of his vision, speaking with the authority lent by a deceased president who had led the nation to victory, was now telling the American people something they had never heard before: Our future as a great nation will depend on our higher education institutions. The direct recipient of this colossal mandate was a man generally acknowledged by many of his peers to be an uneducated midwestern political journeyman. Truman, the man who now found himself leading the nation and the single most important individual in Bush's grand design for American higher education, had never even attended college.

Truman and Bush did not hit it off. Whatever inclined the Brahmin FDR to have complete faith in his Yankee science and technology advisor did not show up in the relationship with the Missouri-bred "show me" mentality of the new president. Above all, Bush wanted in place a science and technology program that would assure America's continued leadership in the postwar world, and he believed that only America's academic community, left to its own ways, could accomplish this. He also wanted to guarantee a continuous stream of students to ensure the dominance of American research. And by 1944 he knew there would be some additional students—no one could guess how many—coming into our colleges, universities, and graduate schools. America was in for a shock.

10. Thelin, *Essential Documents*, 218–19.

CHAPTER SIX

The Perfect Storm

"It would be inaccurate to suggest that there ever was a 'Golden Age' when most college students were industrious and deeply absorbed in their coursework."

—DEREK BOK, *Higher Education in America*[1]

"In 1947–48, returning veterans made up nearly 50% of all students nationwide. Over half the 20,000 undergraduates at Michigan were returning veterans. By 1949, 2½ million students were in college, more than a million more than in any pre-war year."

—CHRISTOPHER P. LOSS, *Between Citizens and the State*[2]

THE G.I. BILL: WHAT NO ONE SAW COMING

If it weren't for the G.I. Bill, 1945–46 might have passed as a seamless return to the pre-war United States of America. Southern Democrats continued to control the Congress. Jim Crow was alive and well in the South, and de Tocqueville's observation that "nowhere is [America]

1. (Princeton: Princeton University Press, 2013), 183.
2. (Princeton: Princeton University Press, 2012), 114.

more intolerant than in those states where slavery was never known" was still accurate a century later. In the South, incidents of lynching and beating started up as soon as Black veterans returned home. In the North, government-funded housing developments like Levittown were for whites-only occupancy. As for gender, Rosie the Riveter was thanked for her war efforts and told that it was time to return to the kitchen. Even if we had won the war thanks to a handful of non-Anglo-Saxon refugees, the campus quotas based on race, religion, or ethnicity reminded higher education observers that diversity was not a priority for university leaders, students, or faculty. The Good Guys had won the war, and that's how the story could be told. We would conveniently forget eugenics, drop Charles Lindbergh with the America First movement down a hole, and still maintain our immigration policies, college quotas, and the unanimity and homogeneity of the overwhelmingly white, Protestant, and male university community. The American historical narrative was still in "safe hands." One might fairly ask: How much of the 1930s would still be evident in the America of the postwar 1940s? Colleges and universities, right up to America's unexpected involvement in World War II, maintained much of the character and makeup of faculties and students from the previous century. Even the philanthropists, eager to create a new kind of university, kept to the Christian traditions of an earlier America. President Gilman of Johns Hopkins had spoken of an "Enlightened Christianity" as the foundation of his new university. Was there any reason to expect postwar America to be any different from pre-war America?

One piece of legislation produced dramatic unforeseen consequences that changed the nation forever. When Congress passed the G.I. Bill, in 1944, it set in motion—however unintentionally—the greatest unplanned educational revolution in American history. The legislation was initiated in the hope that the conflicts over unemployment, which returning veterans experienced after World War I, could be avoided by enticing troops to head to the college campus. Experts anticipated, at best, a modest increase of a few hundred thousand in college admissions. One of the principal sponsors of the law was the American Legion, not a force favoring social disruption.

The expected trickle turned into a tidal wave of returning G.I.'s flocking to higher education. By 1946 more than a million had enrolled, and by 1950 two million, more than doubling the number of college and university enrollments of the immediate pre-war period. This was the first sudden, unanticipated consequence of the G.I. Bill. "The expansion came without preparation, almost without awareness,"[3] wrote the historians Oscar and Mary Handlin in a report for the Carnegie Foundation for the Advancement of Teaching in 1970. To the complete surprise of most campus administrators, these older

---

3. *The American College and American Culture: Socialization as a Function of Higher Education* (New York: McGraw-Hill, 1970).

students—many married and with families—turned out to be an extraordinarily driven new wave: eager, focused, mature, and economically and ethnically more diverse. They represented an untapped pool of American talent. Unprepared campuses found themselves racing to make family housing available; Quonset huts, dilapidated faculty accommodations, and any available temporary shelter was improvised for the returning G.I.s, their brides, and their infants.[4]

These were not the typical college applicants. Even with racial restrictions and ethnic quota systems still in place, many of these battle-hardened veterans were not about to knock gently on the doors of elite American academic institutions, asking politely for admission. A million veterans had brought back war brides. The government had made promises, and the returning G.I.s expected delivery. But America in 1946 was not yet ready for certain kinds of change.

Black G.I.'s faced the highest hurdles. Many states still had anti-miscegenation laws. Southern public and private universities continued to exclude Black applicants until the Civil Rights Movement prodded government intervention a decade later. No accredited engineering or science doctoral programs were available to Black students in the South. The military had fought World War II under Jim Crow restrictions, and only Harry Truman's executive order officially ended segregation in the military

4. Hollywood, as always, reflects the American mood. See https://www.nytimes.com/1948/10/16/archives/apartment-for-peggy-superior-film-written-directed-by-george-seaton.html.

in 1948, although it continued for years. The G.I. Bill, which also included assistance in acquiring low-cost mortgages for home purchases, was interpreted to limit access on campuses or communities to returning Black veterans.[5] Baseball, the "national pastime," was ready to resume the postwar "whites-only" game until the Brooklyn Dodgers' owner Branch Rickey and an aggressive, recently discharged Army lieutenant named Jackie Robinson took on the other fifteen major league owners as well as the majority of players, who wanted no change. Complete integration of organized baseball took another decade. The last team to bring a Black ballplayer to the Major Leagues was the Boston Red Sox in 1959, twelve years after Robinson broke the color barrier. Housing was the same story. Between 1947 and 1951 William Levitt built his planned community on Long Island with federal funding. *Time* ran a story in the summer of 1950 praising Levittown as "a new way of life." The purchase protocol agreement reminded new owners that it was forbidden to rent or sell to persons "other than members of the Caucasian race."[6]

The white ethnic veterans—including the earlier despised eastern European and southern Mediterranean peoples who had been singled out for exclusion in the restrictive immigration laws of the 1920s, such as Jews,

5. See Ira Katznelson, *When Affirmative Action Was White: An Untold History of Racial Inequality in Twentieth-Century America* (New York: W. W. Norton, 2006).

6. See Richard Rothstein, *The Color of Law: A Forgotten History of How Our Government Segregated America* (New York: Liveright, 2017), 69–86.

Italians, Armenians, and Greeks—now came to Harvard, Michigan, North Carolina, Berkeley, and to small colleges all over the country. They majored in every conceivable academic discipline, many in science, many in the humanities and social sciences. Jews and Catholics, until recently limited by quotas and singled out for intimidation and exclusion by a revitalized northern KKK in the 1920s and 1930s, now were sought after by admissions personnel looking for much-wanted tuition dollars, having grown accustomed to government money during the war years when training students for the Reserve Officers' Training Corps (ROTC). Federal stipends were enticing, addictive, and increasingly important, and the G.I.s came with the government's money. The colleges and universities saw the handwriting on the wall and wanted the income, and in the decade after the end of the war, the ethnic quotas gradually disappeared. Since many of the new students arrived with woeful secondary school preparation, the colleges quickly instituted even more remedial programs than those needed for earlier applicants. By 1947 the federal government was supplying one-third of all operating revenue of higher education institutions.[7]

The entrenched traditional academic community initially had no idea of the consequences for their profession. For the existing faculty, especially in the bastions of Protestant orthodoxy, many of the returning G.I.s spoke a different intellectual language. The scientific community had seen what the immigrants from Europe

7. Handlin and Handlin, *The American College and American Culture*, 73.

brought to their research laboratories. They and their offspring could not be kept out of a modern intellectual meritocracy any longer. Now a first generation born in America—many of the veterans were the children of immigrants—raced through their college degrees, and many kept going on to graduate school and doctorates in science, technology, engineering, mathematics, social sciences, and the humanities. The tidal wave of war veterans in undergraduate degree programs had created a shortage of faculty, and this ready-and-willing cohort moved right into place, waiting to join the few thousand older émigré colleagues, who earlier had found a hard-fought acceptance.

Some disciplines did not like what they were seeing. In history and English departments, the most traditional and resistant to change, worry and an unhappiness soon began to express themselves in despair. In his address at the American Historical Association's annual meeting at the Conrad Hilton Hotel in Chicago on December 29, 1962, Carl Bridenbaugh, university professor at Brown and outgoing association president, expressed a bitterness that reflected how the G.I. Bill had fundamentally changed an academic discipline and the collegial world to which he had become accustomed: "It is my duty as your President to report on the state of the profession and to suggest tentatively some measures to be taken for the benefit of ourselves and our posterity."[8] He then launched into a characterization of the academic environment

8. Carl Bridenbaugh, "The Great Mutation," *The American Historical Review* 68 (1963), 315–31.

in American history that he described as "high tragedy," almost "the crumbling of a civilization round and about me. . . . Today we must face the discouraging prospect that we all, teachers and pupils alike, have lost much of what the earlier generation possessed, *the priceless asset of a shared culture*" (my italics). Fifteen years after the end of World War II, this distinguished American historian looked back on a tradition in American higher education that was shaped in the countryside, villages, and small towns, and on the frontier of colonial America and across the expansion of the United States. This "shared culture" had remained intact, firmly in the hands of teachers and scholars trained in a common cause and common vision, whether they came from the North or South. After the Civil War, as American history moved westward, historians wrote books that chronicled the destiny of a nation, and they shared a common core, the same sentiment expressed by T. S. Eliot and the Southern Agrarians: the recognition that a "native" American tradition had taken root in what was to become in pre–World War II an acceptance of a distinct and unique American experience. Different folks need not apply.

It was the academic historians who above all others spoke for the shared narrative of American history, who took the responsibility to speak for the essential common "soul" that reflected the American experience. George Bancroft (1800–1891) and Frederick Jackson Turner (1861–1932) trained and educated generations of historians to identify the destiny of a nation carved from a wilderness and moving a frontier. Few earlier academic historians had challenged the accepted narrative; before World War I, Columbia's Charles A. Beard had taken on the establishment view of American history, had his patriotism questioned, and resigned—but most American historians agreed that the nation's narrative was safe in their hands.

Now, in the early 1960s, outgoing President Bridenbaugh, in a speech he titled "The Great Mutation," saw the end of that tradition of shared values. There was a new generation entering the profession: "the urban-bred scholars of today." In history and English departments all over America, the ethnic landscape was changing. So was American culture—Emerson, Melville, Hawthorne, Dickinson, Whitman, Twain, James, Faulkner, and Hemingway were giving ground to Bellow, Malamud, Roth, Baldwin, and Hansberry.

Within a few years, the first Asian-American and Latin-American courses were being offered. In history departments, specialists in American immigration, ethnicity, Native American studies, and the march to the frontier were offering courses with a very different perspective. Even baseball became a legitimate subject.[9] The war for the soul of America was about to begin on campus.

9. In 1956 Cornell's history department awarded the first doctorate on baseball, "Baseball to 1890: The Early Years," to Harold Seymour, who had been a batboy for the Brooklyn Dodgers, later a worshipful fan of Jackie Robinson. In 1960 Oxford University Press published Seymour's book and became the first academic publisher of a book on baseball.

For historians like Professor Bridenbaugh, these new forces represented a breakup of their familiar world. He held out hope for a continuity of tradition: "The finest historians will not be those who succumb to the dehumanizing methods of social sciences, whatever their uses and values, which I hasten to acknowledge. Nor will the historian worship at the shrine of that Bitch-goddess, QUANTIFICATION" (Bridenbaugh's emphasis). These "urban bred scholars of today" were about to change the face of the American faculty forever.

THE TRUMAN COMMISSION REPORT

The impact of the G.I. Bill stunned the campuses. And it was the high school–graduate president who pushed hardest for the veterans. In the summer of 1946, Truman appointed a presidential commission, consisting of twenty-eight educators from all over the country, to talk about a topic that was not even mentioned in the American Constitution: the national government's role in education. By the end of the following year, the commission produced a massive six-volume document that for the first time opened the door for federal involvement—and resources—in American colleges and universities. The commission included the broad areas of education in America from K–12 and onward but the emphasis was clear from its title: *Higher Education for American Democracy*.

Truman's action bore the fingerprints of Bush's *Science: The Endless Frontier*, but the mandate to the commission went beyond anything previously seen on the topic of education. Bush wanted the colleges and universities to provide the pathway for new scientific knowledge for those gifted enough to single-mindedly advance to the highest levels of scientific and technical achievement. He laid out a minimum of six years to get a student from college to doctoral degree and ready for research. But Truman, with his roots in a segregated state, accepted the responsibility that all Americans should have equal opportunities that only a desegregated system could provide. (Two dissenting southern state members of the commission did not sign the report.) Bush was interested in science and technology and gave lip service to other disciplines; the Truman Commission took on issues related to "demographics, civil rights, social justice, economic opportunity, and the growing belief in access to a college education as an important, perhaps indispensable passport" for the future of all Americans.[10] This was the first clarion call: a college education for all. The proposals were revolutionary. More than a decade before Clark Kerr and the California Plan, the Truman Commission advocated forcefully for a minimum general two-year community college education for everyone, for universal education in a democracy, without gender or racial bias.

The Truman Commission's recommendations were dependent on the largesse of a Congress that was still very much in the hands of conservative legislators. Southern

10. Thelin, *Essential Documents*, 225.

Democrats with seniority controlled the purse strings of the nation when it came to education—which, until the G.I. Bill, was exclusively in the hands of the states—and they were not about to fund desegregated educational opportunity for all. "Separate but equal" was still the law of the land. This postwar society was, furthermore, not prepared to accept women on equal footing. They had made an enormous contribution to the war effort, and they were about to enter an educational environment that offered little change from that before the war. Some historians propose a beginning date of 1945 for the Golden Age of American higher education, but indicators show that the nation was not yet ready in the immediate postwar years to accept the changes required in American society to make much higher educational headway. The G.I. tidal wave was just gathering force. Admissions offices, which had not changed their policies regarding traditional secondary school applicants, initially expected business as usual, as it was anticipated in so much of American life.[11]

THE RESEARCH SUPERCHARGERS: THE NSF AND NIH

Science: The Endless Frontier was one man's blueprint for the future of the American university. But while no one

---

11. The following book title generally reflects the attitude of the time on all-male campuses of the most prestigious colleges: Nancy Weiss Malkiel, *"Keep the Damned Women Out": The Struggle for Coeducation* (Princeton: Princeton University Press, 2016).

saw the role that research would play in the postwar era as clearly as Bush, his flinty temperament and stubborn insistence on having his own way delayed the implementation of the vision.

The OSRD was the successor to the NDRC. In 1941, the funding went from FDR's presidential discretionary money to a massive infusion of federal money to support the billions needed for research to win the war. As victory over the Axis Powers grew certain, Bush began planning for a seamless peacetime transition that would guarantee a new paradigm for academic research, something never anticipated before the war. Until 1941, academic research in science and engineering rarely was supported by government dollars. Private foundations and occasionally industry might contribute to campus research labs, but the government and universities were not in business together. That changed with Bush and the OSRD, and when that organization was dissolved in 1947, Bush was ready. He hoped to prepare the nation for a national science foundation that would supercharge academic research and create an elite cadre of institutions that would pick up the mantle of world leadership in scientific research. Bush described it in the summary of the report that he gave to Truman in July 1945: "I recommend that a new agency for these purposes be established. Such an agency should be composed of persons of broad interest and experience, understanding the peculiarities of scientific research and scientific education. It should have stability of funds so that long-range programs may be undertaken. It should recognize that freedom of inquiry must be preserved and should leave internal control of policy, personnel, and the method and scope of research to the institutions in which it is carried on. It should be fully responsible to the President and through him to the Congress for its program."[12]

Bush offered a blunt mandate to accompany the creation of the National Science Foundation (NSF) for the president and the Congress: Hand over the money and get out of the way. He had hoped for a revolution in medical research as well, stimulated by NSF funding. However, when Congress finally got around to creating the agency, it deliberately thwarted Bush's hope for the health sciences. NSF is the only federal agency with a mission statement that specifically includes "support for all fields of fundamental science and engineering, except for medical sciences." He needn't have worried: The National Institutes of Health (NIH) would provide.

For all his spectacular wartime accomplishments, Bush could be very ham-handed. He had enormous respect for academic brilliance, worked easily with the finest minds in the scientific world and with the smarter top brass in the military, enjoyed the loyalty of his hand-picked associates in the federal bureaucracies, and had an almost mystical relationship with FDR. But when he had to navigate the halls of Congress and do battle with those even closer to President Truman, some of his personal imperiousness prevented or delayed his

12. Thelin, *Essential Documents*, 224.

dream for science. For nearly five years, Bush refused to compromise in his insistence that academic researchers be left almost totally independent and free from excessive (at least in Bush's mind) oversight. The congressional leadership wanted no part of an enormous academic expansion without appropriate government oversight. President Truman vetoed one bill and Congress buried several others, until finally, in 1950, Truman signed a bill that established the NSF.

Bush got most of the freedom from oversight that he wanted for the American research universities. But Congress got its revenge: The first operational year's appropriation was a paltry $3.5 million, barely one-tenth of what was requested, with a permanent $15 million ceiling. He was so angry at the funding level that he told researchers at the Carnegie Institution in Washington not to bother applying for NSF funding. Above all, he was furious that the final legislation had no medical research component. At the time of the successful Soviet launch of Sputnik in October 1957, its first director, Alan Waterman, was still serving as the head of the NSF, described years later by the official foundation historian as "an insignificant agency." Ten years after the end of World War II, the full force of NSF-funded scientific investigation had not yet been evident. Sputnik changed all of that. As discussed above, the G.I. Bill eventually would produce an enormous increase in the number and diversity of undergraduate and graduate students, which within a decade would result in a formidable crop of young researchers about to enter the academic scientific and technological work force. On top of this were the increasing numbers of foreign-born scientist-refugees and immigrants from the 1930s on who had escaped Fascist tyranny.

Once the spigot of government funding was turned on, the transformation of American research universities that had begun gradually in the mid-1930s with a slow stream of refugees took a dramatic turn. In the fiscal, the year before Sputnik, the NSF budget had reached at $40 million. For fiscal 1959, it more than tripled to $134 million, and by 1969 the Congress allocated nearly $500 million for NSF-funded projects, overwhelmingly granted to American research universities and including enormous capital funding for programs designed to build research infrastructure on American campuses. In 1990 the NSF federal appropriation passed $2 billion, a significant portion of which was dedicated to basic research and, irrespective of Bush's hopes, to non-medical-related activities.

Bush's insistence on giving the academic scientists significant control over allocation and project review put enormous power in the hands of university faculty. During the presidency of Lyndon Johnson in the mid-1960s, the accumulated forces of funding, new faculty, and an abundance of graduate students propelled American university research beyond anything that the rest of the world could accomplish. Only the American academic research community could deliver on President John F. Kennedy's promise in 1961 to put a man on the moon by the end of the decade. When Neil Armstrong placed his foot on the moon in 1969, except for a few

German rocket experts who had fled the ruins of Germany, the overwhelming number of engineers and scientists in the Houston Control Center and Cape Canaveral were products of government-funded American graduate programs.

The health sciences need not have worried. Their "Golden Age" was truly spectacular: They had the NIH.

THE NATIONAL INSTITUTES
OF HEALTH

In *Science: The Endless Frontier*, Bush proposed a revolution in American medical research. He envisioned an enormous funding machinery to provide a previously unimaginable amount of financial support for generations of American researchers, their laboratories, facilities, buildings, and anything else they would need. All this treasure would be placed at the disposal of the scientists themselves to push the frontiers of discovery into new uncharted territory. While Bush had wanted the NSF to provide the umbrella, it instead fell to the government's public-health arm, the National Institute of Health, formed in the late 1880s, to become the enormous operation that would advance health and health-related research around the world.

As of 2018 the annual budget of the NIH was $37 billion, nearly five times the size of the NSF. Of all the leaps forward accomplished by the American universities, nothing matched the achievement of the medical schools, academic hospitals, and their associated biomedical and public health research efforts during the postwar decades. It might not have been done in the administrative manner that Bush wanted, but the federal government made more funds available, via grants awarded by peer review committees, than the rest of the world could produce in the half-century after the end of World War II. From its start as a modest federal public health facility, the NIH exploded into a research engine with twenty-seven institutes and centers of different biomedical disciplines. The NIH focus on health and disease did not ignore basic research, and scientists from all over the world were drawn to American universities for research opportunities that simply were not available anywhere else. The decisions on funding were, to a considerable extent, left to review panels of the most eminent scientists in the country. This reflected Bush's faith that the researchers understood—unlike laymen, the Congress, or private industry that expected results advantageous to a targeted application—just how risky and essential basic research was.[13]

The 1960s and 1970s were truly the Golden Age for biomedical researchers in America.[14] Money also poured

13. Senator William Proxmire's Golden Fleece Award (1975–88) epitomized what Bush and others feared when public officials ridiculed selective federally funded, basic research projects for which they saw no merit or application and, as far as they were concerned, served no purpose other than to squander public money.

14. Putting a finger exactly on when constitutes a Golden Age has never been easy. Steven Brint, in *Two Cheers for Higher Education: Why American Universities Are Stronger Than Ever—and How to Meet*

into research facility programs to provide grants for the cost of constructing, remodeling, and equipping laboratories at American medical schools and teaching hospitals. Over the decades since the end of the war, thousands of principal investigators, postdoctoral fellows, and researchers have benefited from the funding provided by the NIH, the largest biomedical research institution in the world.

American higher education achievement was propelled by a perfect storm. As the second half of the twentieth century folded into the first decades of the twenty-first, the American research university had attained a level of excellence that dominated every objective critical evaluative assessment. Dominance of Nobel Prizes and other international awards tumbled into the faculties of American academic institutions. Nobel dominance did not cease in the new century. Since 2000 Americans have taken home 23 of 38 Nobel Prizes in physics, 20 of 35 in medicine, 24 of 35 in chemistry. That welcome mat to foreign scientists, reluctantly placed on the doorstep of campuses decades ago, was not removed, and by 2007, 56 of the 229 science Nobel Prizes won by Americans had been awarded to foreign-born citizens.[15] As of this writing, the most reliable international rankings continue to

the Challenges They Face (Princeton: Princeton University Press, 2018), insists that the Golden Age for American research is now.

15. See Bret Stephens, "Nobels and National Greatness," *Wall Street Journal*, October 14, 2013.

place 40 American universities in any list of the top-50 research universities in the world.[16]

THE SENATOR FROM ARKANSAS

He represented a former slave state. He even signed the Southern Manifesto, a document that declared the intent of southern lawmakers to oppose desegregation and the Supreme Court's decision in 1954 ending segregation. But J. William Fulbright, the junior senator from Arkansas from 1945 to 1974, might go down in history as the most influential congressional force in higher education since Senator Justin Morrill. His name has become synonymous with international university cooperation.

Fulbright was that rare congressional intellectual who from the start of his career was destined to help create American college and university expansion after World War II. Born in 1906, Fulbright was awarded a Rhodes Scholarship to study at Pembroke College at Oxford University, after a distinguished academic and athletic career at the land-grant University of Arkansas. In 1933 he was elected president of the university, the youngest university president in the country. He began his political life by winning a seat in the U.S. House of Representative

16. See www.shanghairanking.com, "Academic Rankings of World Universities," an annual listing based predominantly on research accomplishments conducted by Shanghai Jiao Tong University in China, Also see: Times Higher Education, https://www.timeshighereducation.com.

and after one term was elected to the first of five six-year terms in the Senate in 1944. He became a significant part of the perfect storm in 1945 when he introduced a bill in Congress that called for using surplus war property to fund American student study abroad. At war's end, there were hundreds of millions of dollars of materiel overseas intended for military use that could help the wrecked economies of Europe, but the staggering European governments had no American dollars. Fulbright proposed that they pay for these goods in their own currency, which then would be distributed to Americans to study at overseas universities. On August 1, 1946, President Truman signed the bill into law, creating the Fulbright Program, which to date has sent nearly 400,000 Americans to study at foreign universities. Because Fulbright applicants were required to have an undergraduate degree, the Fulbright Program fueled a surge in the number of Americans who took the first step toward a graduate education. Many of the returning G.I.s had gotten a taste of life abroad and could not wait to return to Europe with a Fulbright grant providing enough francs, lira, Deutschmarks, British pounds, and other exotic currencies to live modestly for a year as a civilian student.

For many, the Fulbright year was the beginning of a commitment to the academic life. Fifty-nine Fulbright scholars went on to win Nobel Prizes; thousands continued studying for the doctorate, another part of the perfect storm.

CLARK KERR AND NELSON ROCKEFELLER

It was not only the elite research universities—both public and private—that underwent a revolution in the immediate postwar period. Almost every state responded to some extent to the unforeseen consequences of the G.I. Bill, some more quickly than others. New York and California, both of which had the benefit of a visionary leader for higher education, created transformative higher educational systems.

Clark Kerr (1911–2003) was, like a dozen earlier American university presidents in the nineteenth century, an agent for fundamental change. His undergraduate college was Swarthmore, and his graduate degrees were from Stanford and the University of California, Berkeley, where he earned a doctorate in economics. After a few years at the University of Washington he returned to Berkeley and was named its first chancellor when the position was created in 1952. In 1958 he was appointed president of the entire University of California system and during the next nine years was a major force in propelling American higher education to a new place. He was the architect of the California Master Plan for Higher Education in 1960, which cemented the position of the two great flagship campuses at Berkeley and Los Angeles (UCLA) at the top of the California pyramid. They were, from the beginning, acknowledged as the pinnacle of the California research universities, producers of faculty for the nation, and with resources now pouring in, they guaranteed their place in the research life of America and the world, a position they continue to hold today, despite periods of stress and strain. Kerr also envisioned another tier of research university and targeted the under-resourced campuses at Irvine, Davis, Santa Barbara, and Riverside for research expansion with the addition of doctorate-level graduate education. They would become part of the research agenda for California higher education. He then proposed to expand the California State University system, an elevation of the old normal schools, state teachers colleges, and state colleges into a system of what today are twenty-three state university campuses spread throughout the length and breadth of California.[17] Finally, completing his plan for universal higher education, Kerr proposed dozens of community colleges, which would guarantee admission to anyone seeking the first rung on the ladder of post-secondary higher education. The two-year community college would also serve as a stepping stone to the institutions above them.

Despite the occasional chaos, confusion, relentless criticism, admissions scandals, and political and financial struggles in the state of California over the next sixty years, no one has been able to tear down what Kerr built. This one state—the seventh-largest economy in the world—created a model of public, universal higher

17. At one Modern Language Association convention in Chicago in 1962, representatives of the California state universities at Humboldt, Stanislaus, Heyward, Sonoma, and Northbridge were handing out small tangerine trees with offers of assistant professorships in an effort to recruit faculty. Almost every graduate student who attended this convention returned with multiple offers of employment in California.

education unlike anything previously imagined. As of 2018 the California community college system of higher education, with 2.1 million students attending 114 colleges, is the largest system in the country. And it will always be associated with the name of this one visionary.

On the other side of the country, 3,000 miles away, a similar transformation was occurring. Nelson Rockefeller was governor of New York State from 1959 to 1973, and at almost the same time that Kerr was bringing about a revolution in California public higher education, Rockefeller was determined to start a similar disruption in New York. He inherited a mediocre and disorganized system of generally undistinguished colleges and universities desperately in need of both physical and academic upgrading. One of his first acts was the creation of a State University Construction Fund that eventually spent over $2 billion in rebuilding campuses all over the state. Between 1959 and 1961 Rockefeller signed legislation that ignited a fire under the moribund public system established in 1948 and gave new meaning to its iconic description: The State University of New York (SUNY). Sleepy campuses in upstate New York—in Potsdam, New Paltz, Oneonta, Fredonia, Plattsburgh, and dozens of other locations—were given instructions by the governor's office in Albany: Go get students and hire faculty. [18]

18. It was not unusual for graduate students within a year or even two of the final degree, returning from the academic conventions in the early 1960s and having placed their names on an interview list, to find a

New York's organizational structure was remarkably similar to that of California but without the top layer of great research universities such as those at Berkeley and Los Angeles. Cornell University, a hybrid institution privately created in 1865 by the American philanthropist Ezra Cornell but given land-grant status, was still viewed for the most part as a private research university. The fully state-operated research institutions would have to be constructed almost from the bottom up, designated for campuses at Binghamton, Stony Brook, and Buffalo. The comprehensive universities, which had grown out of the old normal schools and teachers' colleges, were in place. The community college system could be rebuilt on the current base. But world-class research universities took time to build. So Rockefeller took another bold step in April 1961, when he signed into law legislation merging the resources of four New York City colleges (City College of New York, Hunter, Brooklyn, and Queens) with a new name that it would carry into the future: CUNY, the City University of New York.

California and New York represented the two largest expansions affecting the job market for faculty in the early 1960s. But in between the two oceans, most colleges and universities were also experiencing the effects of the G.I. Bill, the availability of federal dollars, the

---

dozen letters from California and New York seeking further information about their current or future availability.

pressure for expansion, the shortage of faculty, and, inevitably, a changing of the old guard academic community, as ethnic admissions quotas disappeared and acceptance of immigrant faculty became more general all over the country. Colleges petitioned state agencies to amend their founding charters and change their names so that they would become known as universities. Higher education in America had become an extraordinary growth industry as measured by any international standard. Nobel Prizes and worldwide recognition of American academic achievement, even if driven by immigrant scientists, could not be denied. By the late 1950s the Golden Age of higher education in America was underway. Most Americans were unaware of it, an ever-growing number of skeptics simply could not believe it, and many just didn't care.

The Golden Age was short-lived. By the late 1970s there was already talk of a great academic depression. The search for prestige had led to an explosion of Ph.D. programs and a resulting glut. Peter Novick characterized the end of the great job market at colleges and universities as "a crisis of overproduction."[19] But for those of us who experienced the exhilaration of a nationwide opportunity to make a career on a campus, it was a unique moment.

19. *That Noble Dream: The "Objectivity Question" and the American Historical Profession* (Cambridge: Cambridge University Press, 1988), 574.

CHAPTER SEVEN

Beyond Belief

A Refusal to Accept the Honor

"Every generation on the lookout for evidence
of precipitous educational decline has had no
problem finding it."

—CHRISTOPHER P. LOSS, "Past Imperfect,"
The Chronicle of Higher Education, July 19, 2015

When the Soviet Union orbited the first artificial earth
satellite on October 4, 1957, the achievement was described as "a sobering symbol of Soviet genius" and a
tribute to Soviet universities' research success.[1] There
was a national tendency to fault the American educational system for losing the Cold War to the USSR. The
American way of life, declared Dr. Elmer Hutchisson,
director of the American Institute of Physics, "may be
doomed to rapid extinction." Admiral Hyman Rickover,
head of the Navy's nuclear program, urged American

1. See Barbara Barksdale Clowse, *Brainpower for The Cold War: The
Sputnik Crisis and National Defense Act of 1958* (Westport, Conn.: Greenwood, 1981), 3–35.

educational institutions to "imitate the Russians." Sputnik proved, and a large portion of the nation believed, that American colleges and universities had hopelessly fallen behind.

More than half a century later, in his State of the Union Speech on January 25, 2011, President Barack Obama announced to the nation, "This is our Sputnik moment." Pointing to investments made by China and India, he echoed the theme of an American decline, this time pointing to the failure of our academic institutions to meet the Asian challenge. As far as the American public was concerned, higher education was off the rails and failing the country.[2] Even the American scientific community sounded gloomy. The Fogarty International Center of the NIH released a paper in 2014 with the ominous title "America Is Losing Biomedical Research Leadership to Asia."[3] Four years later the *Wall Street Journal* made it

2. See Karin Fischer and *The Chronicle of Higher Education*, "Inside One City's Love-Hate Relationship with Higher Ed," November 2, 2018. More optimistically, Joseph S. Nye, Jr., in *Is the American Century Over?* (Malden, Mass.: Polity, 2015), suggests that America might continue its hegemony, but under very different terms. Parag Khanna, in *The Future Is Asian* (New York: Simon and Schuster, 2019), points to an inevitable Asian triumph. The *Economist* explains "How China Could Dominate Science" (January 12, 2019, print edition). Robert A. Rhoads, Xiaoyang Wang, Xiaoguang Shi, and Yongcai Chang, in *China's Rising Research Universities: A New Era of Global Ambition* (Baltimore: Johns Hopkins University Press, 2014), believe that China's global ambitions will be fulfilled. Yet one encounters the occasional optimist. See Michael Beckley, *Unrivalled: Why America Will Remain the World's Sole Superpower* (Ithaca: Cornell University Press, 2018).

3. *Global Health Matters Newsletter*, January–February 2014, Vol. 13, issue 1.

official: "U.S. Grip on the Market for Higher Education Is Slipping."[4]

In the more than sixty years between Sputnik and President Obama's remarks, no amount of worldwide success on the part of American science or the nation's ability to attract scholars and students from all over the world to our campuses could alter the perception of the American people. When it came to American colleges and universities, only Alabama football and Duke basketball represented excellence. In 1996 Lawrence Levine made a list of the best-known books on contemporary higher education published in the most recent decade. The titles tell you all you need to know about how matters stood at the close of the twentieth century:

1. *The Closing of the American Mind: How Higher Education Has Failed Democracy and Impoverished the Souls of Today's Students*

2. *ProfScam: Professors and the Demise of Higher Education*

4. Michelle Hackman and Douglas Belkin, December 20, 2018. To understand the current American obsession with China's challenge, see, among many more, Yong Zhao, *Who's Afraid of the Big Bad Dragon?: Why China Has the Best (and Worst) Education System in the World* (San Francisco: Jossey-Bass, 2014); Rhoads et al., *China's Rising Research Universities*; Parag Khanna, *The Future Is Asian* (New York: Simon and Schuster, 2019). America's only hope lay in copying everyone else. See Marc S. Tucker, ed., *Surpassing Shanghai: An Agenda for American Education Built on the World's Leading Systems* (Cambridge: Harvard Education Press, 2011).

3. *The War Against the Intellect: Episodes in the Decline of Discourse*

4. *Tenured Radicals: How Politics Has Corrupted Our Higher Education*

5. *Killing the Spirit: Higher Education in America*

6. *The Hollow Men: Politics and Corruption in Higher Education*

7. *Illiberal Education: The Politics of Race and Sex on Campus*

8. *The De-Valuing of America: The Fight for Our Culture and Our Children*

9. *Imposters in the Temple: American Intellectuals Are Destroying Our Universities and Cheating Our Students of Their Future*

10. *Dictatorship of Virtue: Multiculturalism and the Battle for America's Future*

Had he known of an impending publication by Harvard University Press, Levine could have added Professor Bill Readings's *The University in Ruins* (1996).

This sentiment continued into the first two decades of the twenty-first century:

1. *Higher Education? How Colleges Are Wasting Our Money and Failing Our Kids*

2. *Academically Adrift: Limited Learning on College Campuses*

3. *Excellent Sheep: The Miseducation of the American Elite and the Way to a Meaningful Life*

4. *Fail U.: The False Promise of Higher Education*

5. *The Case Against Education: Why the Education System Is a Waste of Time and Money*

6. *The Lowering of Higher Education in America: Why Student Loans Should Be Based on Credit Worthiness*

7. *Cracks in the Ivory Tower: The Moral Mess of Higher Education*

The authors of this last title, published by Oxford University Press in 2019, reflected the general perception of American colleges and universities: "We think that higher education suffers from serious moral flaws . . . Most academic marketing is semi-fraudulent, grading is largely nonsense, students don't study or learn much, students cheat frequently . . . professors and administrators waste students' money and time in order to line their own pockets."[5]

How do we explain this view among a broad cross-section of Americans that higher education in the United States since the end of World War II has been a failure and even an existential threat to the nation? Most

5. Jason Brennan and Phillip Magness, 3.

Americans are either unaware of or indifferent to the fact that English, the most widely spoken method of communication in the history of civilization, has become the dominant language of research and even instruction in universities all over the world, mainly because of the achievements of American academic institutions. Yet we have come to accept the mediocrity of our colleges and universities almost as an article of faith. Regardless of the evidence of accomplishment, we seem to prefer an image of failure and reports of scandal.

For most of its history, few cared, because few participated, at least until the Morrill Land Grant Act created a viable public university system in the second half of the nineteenth century and gradually more young people were attending post-secondary schools. But higher education, in spite of the Gilded Age commitment of the philanthropists, remained a sideshow for Americans, something experienced by a handful of elite Easterners or the children of citizens who didn't need to keep their sons home either to harvest fields or run the family business.

As the nineteenth century ended, most undergraduate institutions accepted almost anyone who applied. Initially, that included the eager children of the immigrant waves, but soon their numbers caused problems, and the quotas arrived. In the 1920s, when the immigration doors were shut and the private campuses were closed to all but a small percentage and narrow range of the immigrants' offspring, there was little public concern. The policies suited most Americans, and no one cared that much about what was happening on the campuses anyway. In the 1930s restricted immigration, indifference to the rise of Fascism and the plight of its victims, the reborn power of the KKK, the rise of eugenics, and the depth of racial discrimination in the United States were not subjects that were hotly debated—or debated at all—by college students or faculty across the country.[6] What Americans wanted from their colleges and universities was what Hollywood confirmed. When critics like Thorstein Veblen, Robert Hutchins, Upton Sinclair, or Abraham Flexner, in the years just before America's entry into the world war, described what they perceived as the mediocrity of American higher education and the superiority of the Europeans, Americans shrugged their shoulders and went to the movies to cheer on the football players.

During the past half-century, however, the attention of the American people has been drawn to higher education in a wholly unanticipated way. By the second decade of the twenty-first century, it was not unusual to see three university-related stories in the *Wall Street Journal*, *New York Times*, or *Washington Post*, all unflattering. In the May 2, 2019, edition of the *Journal*, for example, three typical stories appeared in the first section: one on

6. See, besides Kevles and Okrent, Edwin Black, *War Against the Weak: Eugenics and America's Campaign to Create a Master Race* (New York: Thunder's Mouth, 2003); Jonathan Peter Spiro, *Defending the Master Race: Conservation, Eugenics, and the Legacy of Madison Grant* (Burlington: University of Vermont Press, 2009). Every generation seems to have its own version of "political correctness," followed by the next generation's amnesia. The American academic community's embrace of eugenics, however, led to public policy legislation of enormous dimensions. It is arguable that academic eugenics made possible the restrictive immigration laws and government-mandated sterilization in the decades before World War II.

"admissions fraud," explaining how a family paid more than $6 million to get a child into Stanford; a second on bribes to college basketball coaches "that exposed the seedy underbelly of college basketball"; and the third, a review of a book entitled *The Adjunct Underclass*[7], which describes the exploitation of part-time adjunct faculty on campuses "where college teaching has become a pick-up job like driving for Uber."[8] Higher education had become big news, and it was generally all bad.

Colleges had provided a shot of adrenaline and drama for the struggling print newspaper industry. On May 5, 2019, three days after the *Wall Street Journal* stories, the "Ethicist" column in the Sunday *New York Times Magazine*, by the American academic philosopher Kwame Anthony Appiah, featured this moral dilemma submitted by a young reader: "Almost All the Colleges I Wanted to Go to Rejected Me. Now What?" The timing was perfect. For the previous three months the *Times*, along with most every other media outlet in the country, had been running stories about the scandals of parents who tried to bribe their way into admissions for their children in prestigious colleges. Another higher education story in the same day's *Times* offered a full-page narrative with

7. Herb Childress, *The Adjunct Underclass: How America's College Betrayed Their Faculty, Their Students, and Their Mission* (Chicago: University of Chicago Press, 2019).

8. Melissa Korn and Jennifer Levitz, "Family Paid $6.5 Million for Stanford Shot," A6; Andrew Beaton and Rebecca Davis O'Brien, "How Not to Bribe a College Basketball Coach," A14; Barton Swaim, "Teachable Moments," A15.

a despairing photo and headline across the entire page: "Hunger on Campus: Pay Tuition or Eat."[9]

After centuries of public indifference, higher education in America, even in the midst of its greatest success and global dominance, with students from all over the world eager for a place on almost *any* campus, had developed a profound image problem. This "perfect storm" has left Americans inside and outside the academic world with conflicting realities. Just how bad—or how good— were we? It had taken a campus revolution to focus our attention on this question.

The explosions of the late 1960s did not happen in a vacuum. They had unexpected and disruptive antecedents. Like Branch Rickey and Jackie Robinson, the Warren Supreme Court was an anomaly on matters of race from 1953 to 1969, until Chief Justice Earl Warren retired and was replaced by Warren Burger. Who, after all, expected racial justice to be championed by Eisenhower's nominee Warren, the former California attorney general who had advocated separating Americans of Japanese descent from the rest of the population? Yet in *Brown v. Board of Education* in the spring of 1954, the Court overturned its 7-1 decision in *Plessy v. Ferguson* (1896). The Warren Court's opinion arguably did not reflect the attitudes of a majority of Americans any more than Branch Rickey's single-minded resolve to integrate—baseball,

9. Kaya Laterman, "Tuition or Dinner? Nearly Half of College Students Surveyed in a New Report Are Going Hungry," *The New York Times*, May 5, 2019.

opposed by the other fifteen owners and improbably supported by his bourbon-sipping Kentucky-born commissioner of baseball, Albert "Happy" Chandler—reflected a national will. For the next thirteen years after the *Brown* decision, fourteen states still forbade interracial marriage until the Warren Court again, in *Loving v. Virginia* (1967) struck down state anti-miscegenation laws, overturning a previous Supreme Court decision, *Pace v. Alabama*, which had stood since 1883.

The first campus spark was struck in 1964 by a University of California, Berkeley, graduate student in philosophy named Mario Savio. Brought up a devout Catholic in New York City, the son of a Sicilian-born father and first-generation Italian mother, Savio had just returned from Mississippi, where he had worked on Black voter registration. This was the same summer and location where three fellow civil rights workers—James Chaney, Andrew Goodman, and Mickey Schwerner—were murdered. He wanted to fundraise for voter registration and came up against a university policy that forbade political activities of this nature on campus. Savio lit the fuse, and the Berkeley campus exploded; the shock wave spread across the nation from campus to campus.

Savio was only one of thousands of a new kind of student and faculty who had not found a place on many American campuses during the previous century, and now they were ready for a fight. It might have started with the Civil Rights Movement, but America was about to enter a period of loud argument and conflict among its citizenry, and the college and university campuses were destined to be the site of a national shouting match. The

war in Vietnam, women's rights, gender and sexual pref-
erence, race, and economic justice: these were the issues
that generated the fighting words. Between only 1969 and
1970 one heard the music of protest from Woodstock, New
York; witnessed riots at the Stonewall Inn in New York
City to protest police brutality against gays; saw students
shot and killed at Kent State and Jackson State; and observed a national student strike. This was not exactly the
stuff that Groucho's President Wagstaff had expected.

WHO TELLS THE STORY OF AMERICAN
HISTORY AND AMERICAN LITERATURE?

How do we present the past? Whose cultural memory
is privileged to tell the story of the nation? Is there an
authentic American literary heritage? If there is a canon
of American literature, who defines it? By the 1960s
the new generation of historians that Carl Bridenbaugh
had warned about in his presidential lamentation was
beginning to find a foothold as faculty members across
the nation. They had uncovered new research topics
and (previously ignored) subjects offering histories and
literary works that would have had no place in the traditional frontier view of the American past of George
Bancroft and Frederick Jackson Turner.[10] English and

10. One of the first coherent critiques of traditional scholarship in
literature and history was *The Dissenting Academy*, edited by Theodore
Roszak (New York: Random House, 1967). There had been earlier dis-
senters. The historian Charles A. Beard had published *An Economic
Interpretation of the Constitution of the United States* in 1913 and set off
a storm by questioning the motives of the Founding Fathers. Many of
his colleagues thought it was an act of near treason to suggest that class

history departments, having run out of a reliable supply of white Protestant men, found themselves looking at applicant pools that contained women and individuals with surnames rarely encountered in previous departmental faculty searches.[11] When the students began their protests for change, for the first time there was a new faculty presence on campus ready to support them and take up the challenge. History and English departments were the front lines. And the prize for the winners? The ownership of the American historical and literary past. Homogeneity, civility, and consensus were about to give way to nasty argument.

From the outset, it was a bitter conflict. The American Historical Association and the Modern Language Association were immediately embroiled in controversy that streamed out of the campuses and into the presidential campaign of 1968. Here were the ingredients of what became known as the "culture wars," in existential terms "a war for the soul of America" that was destined to be

---

conflict was at the heart of the American dream, and that the Constitution was written to assure the triumph of big business and those who owned property. Such a theory was felt to be "un-American."

11. Lawrence Levine, writing twenty years later, said: "The university is no longer the site of homogeneity in class, gender, ethnicity, and race. In 1960 only 6% of college students were from minority groups; by 1988 the number had risen to almost 30%. In 1960 women earned only 35% of the bachelor's degree and 10% of the Ph.D.'s conferred. In 1990 they earned 54% of the B.A.'s and 37% of the Ph.D.'s. By 1985 27% of the faculty in institutions of higher education were women, and more than 10% were non-White." *The Opening of the American Mind: Canons, Culture, and History* (Boston: Beacon, 1996), xvii.

fought on American campuses from the 1960s to today.[12] History and literature became subjects of controversy that split departments. The movement that some said was necessary to re-balance the teaching of American civilization, which became known as "multicultural- ism," was used both for triumph and derision. A new generation found itself, as Lawrence Levine noted, "on a collision course with the conventional accounts of the American past."[13] In 1986, twenty-four years after Bri- denbaugh's address, outgoing President Carl Degler, dis- tinguished American historian at Stanford, could look back on two decades of confrontation: "Groups and subjects ignored in traditional history suddenly became visible, clamoring for inclusion in a historical frame- work that once had no place for them."[14] He described

12. There have been several books describing "the Culture Wars" that characterize the conflicts on American campuses for the past six decades, including Andrew Hartman, *A War for the Soul of America: A History of the Culture Wars* (Chicago: University of Chicago Press, 2015). See also James Davison Hunter, *Culture Wars: The Struggle to Define America* (New York: Basic Books, 1991), and Joyce Appleby, Lynn Hunt, and Margaret Jacob, *Telling the Truth about History* (New York: W. W. Norton, 1994). The professional organizations became fields of combat. See Jesse Lemisch, *On Active Service in War and Peace: Poli- tics and Ideology in the American Historical Profession* (Toronto: New Hogtown, 1975).

13. *Telling the Truth About History*, 152. See also Lawrence W. Levine, *The Unpredictable Past: Explorations in American Cultural History* (New York: Oxford University Press, 1993), and Gertrude Himmelfarb, *The New History and the Old* (Cambridge: Harvard University Press, 1987). These two historians represent the drawn battle lines.

14. Annual address of the president of the American Historical As- sociation, delivered at Chicago, December 28, 1986. *American Historical Review* 92, no. 1 (February 1987), 1–19.

an American narrative that had "splintered" under the weight of historical information that had formerly been excluded: "We have no clear way of determining how this new knowledge will be integrated into what we call the history of the United States." Within a year, Allan Bloom's *The Closing of the American Mind*[15] would reveal how contentious and enduring this struggle for the American narrative would be. As late as 2018, Jill Lepore was still laying out the terms of the argument in her one-volume American history *These Truths*, which she might have called *Which Truths?*[16]

We had been there before, but the nature of earlier academic conflicts was decidedly different and without much of an audience. As late as the 1930s, many eminent English departments dismissed any discussion of American literature. There was no room for Melville, Twain, Emerson, Whitman, Thoreau, James, or Dickinson. Eventually that canonic battle was quietly won, but a new one would erupt in the 1960s and continue for decades as historical figures and writers such as W.E.B. Du Bois, Frederick Douglass, Zora Neale Hurston, Richard Wright, Maya Angelou, James Baldwin, Maxine Hong Kingston, Amy Tan, and many others of color and diverse ethnicity now sought a place in the canon. The defenders of tradition called them "trendy lightweights" and their inclusion in course syllabi as "curriculum debasement."

15. *The Closing of the American Mind: How Higher Education Has Failed Democracy and Impoverished the Souls of Today's Students* (New York: Simon and Schuster, 1987).

16. *These Truths: A History of the United States* (New York: W. W. Norton & Co., 2019).

The courses involved in this new multiculturalism were called with derision "the hyphenated curriculum" by those traditionalists who believed that Western civilization was under threat from "hyphenated" Americans with hyphenated literature. Jewish-American literature—the fiction of Saul Bellow, Bernard Malamud, Philip Roth, Tilly Olsen, and others—changed the look of course offerings of twentieth-century American literature in many departments. These authors would have much preferred to be accepted as part of the literary tradition of Faulkner or Fitzgerald, but their themes and characters had roots in a different soil, their accents not from Oxford, Mississippi or Long Island, New York—and hence, the hyphenated designation for Jewish-American literature, along with Afro-American, Latino/a- American, Asian-American, and more. Later, Bellow became one of the outspoken critics of courses that had abandoned a literary tradition from which he would have been excluded fifty years earlier.

MEDIA MADE THIS STORM PERFECT: THE *CHRONICLE OF HIGHER EDUCATION* AND *U.S. NEWS & WORLD REPORT*

In 1983 *U.S. News & World Report* was the third-ranking weekly news magazine in America, well behind *Time* and *Newsweek* in weekly sales and subscriptions. *U.S. News* needed help to survive. That help came in the form of an editorial brainstorm that the magazine would publish an issue ranking colleges and universities across the country by undergraduate reputation. The first listing appeared in 1983. The editors put together arbitrary criteria, including endowment, alumni giving, opinions of other college presidents, and more than a dozen other data points that contributed to "the list." Questionnaires were sent out to large numbers of post-secondary institutions all over the country. Remarkably, sensing that something important might be happening and not wanting to be left out, most responded. Actually the editors made two lists: one for undergraduate colleges and another for "universities," although one university appeared on the college list and one college on the university list. Some interest was shown by the public; a second ranking appeared two years later in 1985 and a third in 1987, and by that time Americans were hooked. The annual *U.S. News & World Report* rankings became the most widely anticipated list in the magazine publishing world, and American higher education was changed forever. There soon followed a "rankings industry," with dozens of publications including the *Wall Street Journal* and *London Times* issuing their own higher education prestige ladders and competing methodologies. But *U.S. News*, which had got there first, had discovered the golden goose and how to exploit the American obsession with prestige. It eventually published rankings of hospitals, cars, diets, high schools, law firms, vacations, cruises, and health insurance. Americans have become addicted to rankings.

The rankings also meant that American higher education became a topic of much greater significance for the American public than ever in its history. The pros and cons of this public interest and the impact of the rankings game have been and will be argued for years. The hunt for prestige has been blamed for everything perceived as wrong with American colleges and universities: escalating tuition prices, spurring harmful admission practices, corrupting college presidents and their boards of trustees—encouraging institutions to do anything necessary to boost their rankings.[17] What had previously been limited to the sports page—rankings of the top basketball or football programs in the country by sportswriters—was henceforth applied to academic prestige. Colleges and universities in the 1980s were now officially "big news" across the country. Higher education was making national headlines, and there was money to be made in writing about students and faculty. All that was needed next was a popular trade journal dedicated exclusively to colleges and universities.

That void was filled by the *Chronicle of Higher Education*, which had first appeared in November 1966. Initially it was a stately publication that took a decidedly detached, scholarly, and studious look at the issues affecting the professionals who worked in the field. The front-page of the first issue had a photo of the new MIT president, Howard Johnson, a below-the-fold discussion of federal grants, and a lead article about the anticipated actions of Congress in 1967. The *Chronicle* accepted no advertising, was incorporated as a nonprofit, and had no editorial

17. See Wendy Nelson Espeland and Michael Sauder, *Engines of Anxiety: Academic Rankings, Reputation, and Accountability* (New York: Russell Sage Foundation, 2016).

position. It was supported by grants from the Carnegie Foundation and the Ford Foundation. However, in 1978, the publication was sold to its editors, became a for-profit corporation, started soliciting advertisements, and added an editorial page. It remained a weekly, but it was poised to become much more of a headline-grabbing newspaper than its origins would have predicted. In 1997, with the coming of the Internet, the *Chronicle of Higher Education* became more prominent, and American colleges and universities were in the crosshairs of public interest and a new journalism. The *Chronicle* headlines mimicked the more sensational print media. Scandals, failures, embezzlements, sexual activities from the top to the bottom of the academic world, and campus chaos provided red meat for anyone seeking evidence that the higher education "industry" was *in extremis*. The *Chronicle* became the profession's primary trade journal, with often scorching headlines examining the endless problems that its reporters uncovered on campus. It also produced a cadre of investigative journalists who went on to write muckraking books with titles to match, such as *The End of College*, *There Is Life after College*, and *American Higher Education in Crisis?* Even the tone and titles of books written by traditionally trained academics writing about American colleges and universities and published by university presses picked up on the *Chronicle*'s voice: *Our Underachieving Colleges*, *Academically Adrift*, and *The Fall of the Faculty*.[18]

18. Derek Bok, *Our Underachieving Colleges: A Candid Look at How Much Students Learn and Why They Should Be Learning More*, (Princeton: Princeton University Press, 2008); Richard Arum and Josipa Roksa, *Academically Adrift: Limited Learning on College Campuses* (Chicago:

Johns Hopkins University Press, the oldest continuously operating American university press, published books with titles such as *What Ever Happened to the Faculty?*, *The Future of Academic Freedom*, and *The Rise and Decline of Faculty Governance*,[19] echoing the same anxiety and chaos found in the *Chronicle*'s headlines. *Inside Higher Education*, published exclusively online and tending toward the sensational, told the faculty to get busy: "[These new books argue] that shared governance is under threat, along with the future of American higher education, and professors must take up the fight."[20] Not exactly the tone of disinterested scholarly detachment.

Up to the early 1980s one would have been hard-pressed to find a copy of the *Chronicle of Higher Education* on any administrator's desk. The trustees' office might have had the only university subscription, generally responding to an urgent plea from the journal for financial support. The same could be said of the *U.S. News* college ranking issues of 1983 and 1985. Initially, neither trustees nor presidents were interested. By the end of the decade, matters had changed. Parents were paying

University of Chicago Press, 2010); Benjamin Ginsberg, *The Fall of the Faculty: The Rise of the All-Administrative University and Why It Matters* (New York: Oxford University Press, 2011).

19. Larry G. Gerber, *The Rise and Decline of Faculty Governance: Professionalization and the Modern American University* (Baltimore: John Hopkins University Press, 2014); Henry Reichman, *The Future of Academic Freedom* (Baltimore: John Hopkins University Press, 2019); Mary Burgan, *What Ever Happened to the Faculty?: Drift and Decision in Higher Education* (Baltimore: John Hopkins University Press, 2006).

20. Colleen Flaherty, "Clarion Call," July 29, 2014, https://www.inside highered.com/news/2014/07/29/new-book-argues-faculty-governance -under-threat.

attention. Consulting and search firms, which formerly had exclusively served the needs of corporate America, began to establish "educational practices" in the 1980s, offering their services to help recruit prestigious presidents, improve institutional images, suggest tactics, and plan communications strategies to get a higher ranking.[21] All the perfect storm now needed was newsmakers. The 1980s provided them.

WILLIAM PROXMIRE

In 1957 William Proxmire succeeded Republican Joseph McCarthy as a senator from Wisconsin, and this Democrat served for thirty-two years. When he stepped down in 1989, his reputation rested on two remarkable accomplishments. One was his durability: he had said "present" at 10,252 consecutive roll calls, a Congressional record. The other proved to be the first popular public salvo in the war against higher education. In his first year in the Senate in 1957, Senator Proxmire announced the creation of the "Golden Fleece Award" to inform the public of the waste found in research proposals funded by government agencies. Over the next fifteen years he issued in

21. The first recruiting firm to add educational searches to its corporate activities was Heidrick & Struggles, founded in 1953. Korn Ferry appeared in 1969 and added higher education to its portfolio soon after. Those critics trying to understand what brought on the corporate style in American university governance and the explosion in the salaries of academic administrators might well look to the role of the search firm and the marketing strategists who appeared almost out of nowhere in the last quarter of the twentieth century. Today it would be unusual to find a presidential search that was *not* directed by one of the dozens of executive search firms.

his monthly newsletters 168 "Golden Fleece Awards" se-
lecting "the most outrageous examples of federal waste."
Almost all the "awards" were given to faculty at research
universities across the country. American taxpayers loved
Proxmire's blasts at basic science projects funded by the
NSF and NIH. In an early press release, Proxmire stated
that the American people should be spared "the funding
of this nonsense." Peer-reviewed basic science proposals had always been at the heart of the postwar research
success that drove American science to its world leadership. But Proxmire was able to find proposals that on
their face sounded, to the average American, preposter-
ous. He made headlines, and the always-latent American
anti-intellectualism won the battle for public opinion.
The Golden Fleece awards became a staple of the Congressional process for years. Senator Robert Byrd of West
Virginia declared that the Proxmire award "was as much
a part of the Senate as quorum calls and filibusters."[22]

WILLIAM BENNETT

William Bennett had the biggest stage and the loudest
voice. He had the academic credentials and popular political savvy to speak to a wide audience of traditionalists
who saw the new faculty voices increasingly heard in
department meetings and academic conventions as an
assault on Western civilization. He directed the National
Humanities Center in North Carolina from 1979 to 1981,

22. Richard Severo, "William Proxmire, Senator Who Abhored
Waste, Dies," *New York Times*, December 15, 2005.

was chairman of the National Endowment for the Humanities (NEH) from 1981 to 1985, and from 1985 to 1988 served as secretary of education. From these pulpits, he led a sustained attack on anyone he perceived as challenging traditional values, particularly in English and history departments. As a public intellectual, he was an effective advocate for the Western literary canon, proclaiming the threat to American ideals and nobility posed by the new campus voices of multiculturalism. Bennett tapped into a groundswell of American faith and patriotism. He was also a newsmaker, direct and eminently quotable. "Much of the left-liberal elite despise religious beliefs . . . They are profoundly uncomfortable with religious institutions, and the traditional values they embody."[23] This was not a slam coming from some outraged clergyman. Bennett had attended Williams College and gotten a Ph.D. in political philosophy at the University of Texas and a law degree from Harvard. He had spent years at distinguished colleges and universities and now charged that American educational institutions had weakened the nation at a time when the USSR stood as an existential threat to our survival. His report *A Nation at Risk* (1983) described "a rising tide of mediocrity that threatened our very future as a Nation and a people." Although the report was primarily directed at K–12 education, Bennett made it clear in his public statements that American higher education was the muddled final product of a broken system.

23. *The De-valuing of America: The Fight for Our Culture and Our Children* (New York: Summit, 1992), 213.

Millions of copies of *A Nation at Risk* were spread across the country.

LYNNE CHENEY

Lynne Cheney earned her Ph.D. in eighteenth-century British literature at the University of Wisconsin and wrote a dozen books for adults and children describing the virtues found in American history, the history she believed in: "Without the traditional American narrative, we do to ourselves what an unfriendly nation bent on our own destruction might." She succeeded Bennett as chair of the NEH, serving from 1986 to 1993. At various times in the 1980s she was on most lists of the most-admired women in the United States and made front-page news on several scores: Her husband, Dick Cheney, was a prominent public figure and a political force, especially as vice president to President George W. Bush. Like Bennett, Cheney served as a talk show host and displayed the same easy capacity to deal with the general public. They shared the "destiny" traditions of American history reflected in the view that the Founding Fathers and the Constitution had created an orderly nation that had become a moral model to the world. As it turned out, this was the view that most Americans had come to prefer, and Cheney was one of the public defenders of that view of American values. While her husband served as secretary of defense and she as chair of the NEH, the national pundit George Will described her as "Secretary of Domestic Defense" and characterized American higher education as the enemy of the nation: "The foreign adversaries her husband, Dick, must keep at bay are less dangerous, in the long run, than the domestic forces with which she must deal."[24]

Here we were, in the mid-1980s, in a national debate over the meaning of American history and literature. While Bennett and Cheney had earned their doctorates at prestigious American research universities, they were still outside the academic tent. It took an insider to really get the nation's attention.

ALLAN BLOOM

Bloom was a professor of philosophy at the University of Chicago. His primary interests were the Greek philosophers and the European Renaissance. No one could have expected that Bloom would be the author of a diatribe that would verbalize the anger and animosity toward his fellow stakeholders—faculty and students, primarily—felt by an increasing number of Americans who had recently discovered the colleges and universities in their midst. In 1987 Bloom published *The Closing of the American Mind*, the subtitle of which got the attention of readers: *How Higher Education Has Failed Democracy and Impoverished the Souls of Today's Students*. Bloom's denunciation of the American faculty spent four months on top of the *New York Times* bestseller list and eventually sold over a million copies in hardcover and paperback editions. This erudite and somewhat haughty elitist instantly became the defender of whatever the "Western tradition" had come to mean in the minds of many Americans: the literary and historical

24. Cited in Hartman, *A War for the Soul of America*, 222.

prisms through which European civilization and American history and literature had been examined in classrooms around the nation for centuries. Bloom spoke as the defender of a national identity that held fast to a cherished Western intellectual heritage. He did more than just touch a nerve. He pronounced a declaration of war between higher educational institutions in the United States and the rest of the nation. It was a clarion call, and after seeing the astounding response to Bloom's book, others joined in. Within a year Charles Sykes published his first book, *ProfScam: Professors and the Demise of Higher Education*.[25] The floodgates were opened. Faculty who joined Bloom in defense of an earlier academic tradition and the standards of an earlier curriculum had a new organization, the National Association of Scholars (NAS), founded in 1987 to defend "the western intellectual heritage." As the second decade of the twenty-first century comes to a close, there is no end in sight to this conflict, or the criticism.

TROLLING FOR TROUBLE

American higher education has existed with a target on its back for the past half-century. Yet even with hostile attention turned to campuses since the 1960s, something else came along to really put the glare of national attention on our colleges and universities: the Internet.

This vast digital universe has provided the technological reach as well as the ideological intensity to allow

25. *ProfScam: Professors and the Demise of Higher Education* (Washington: Regnery, 1988).

millions of Americans to find and believe whatever they want about the educational and moral failures of colleges and universities, real or purported. Any attempt to find a disinterested reality in this polarized online universe has been difficult, especially when issues of geopolitics, race, and sensitive issues such as anti-Semitism combine into a lethal cocktail. Take the following website headline that went viral: "Anti-Semitism Soars on U.S. College Campuses" (Adam Kredo, *Washington Free Beacon* online, August 8, 2018). What would our archaeologists of the future make of the status of anti-Semitism on American campuses in the first half of the twenty-first century? An online search would provide over three million sites, sources, and articles stating opinions and providing data. Dozens of lists describe colleges and universities that are the most hostile and unwelcoming to Jewish students, while others rank institutions that are the most friendly and comfortable. The same institution is often on both lists. Similarly, there are lists of colleges hostile to Israel, supportive of the "Boycott Israel" movement, and sites with photos of faculty—many of them Jews—described as anti-Semites. Jewish alumni from all over the country express concern, outrage, and fear at the very moment (of this writing) when the presidents of Yale, Princeton, MIT, Brown, Penn, Cornell, Chicago, and Northwestern are Jews. The former Harvard president, Lawrence Bacow, is religiously Orthodox and had a kosher kitchen in the President's House in Cambridge. Bacow was for ten years the president of Tufts, where he had four mezuzahs—doorpost capsules designating a Jewish household—in his campus home.

Morton Schapiro, president of Northwestern, previously served nine years as president of Williams College, unimaginable in the decades before or after World War II.[26] On all these campuses Jewish students make up at least 20 percent of the student body, and it is a safe guess that the same percentage would apply to faculty. But no numbers, data, or facts can equal the force of online headlines and the cyber-speed that allows them to reach millions of Americans in an instant.

Higher education in America is a topic presented to Americans by a media comfortable with disaster, and it is fair to say that higher education has provided more than enough opportunity. Planes that land safely are not news; planes that crash are. The American public has become accustomed to a diet of failure or corruption on the campuses of our colleges and universities. Since a Supreme Court decision in 2018, legalized sports gambling on intercollegiate contests in basketball and football of Division I institutions has soared into the hundreds of millions of dollars each *month*.[27] In 2019 the U.S. spent more than $73 *billion* on sports as "entertainment," three times what we spend on the space program of NASA. The struggle to control or eliminate the near-professional level of intercollegiate basketball and football has failed, and there is no reasonable hope that the appetite of the American public for college students playing basketball or football will

26. See Benjamin Aldes Wurgaft, *Jews at Williams: Inclusion, Exclusion, and Class at a New England Liberal Arts College* (Hanover, N.H.: University Press of New England, 2013).

27. Alan Blinder, "Can Universities Police Sports Betting? Some Are Trying," *New York Times*, October 22, 2019, B9.

ever change. President Robert Maynard Hutchins tried at the University of Chicago in the 1930s to strike such a blow, but two decades later he despaired, writing, "Intercollegiate athletics has become big business; sometimes it seems the principal business of higher education in America."[28] That was only the beginning. Today, with point spreads from Las Vegas on NCAA-sanctioned football and basketball contests instantly available to the gambling public, and television contracts pouring millions of dollars into university athletic department budgets, the hunt for premier high school athletes whose only purpose is to perform on the playing fields becomes the most vital contest between institutions. Some athletes came to college just long enough to display their talents and sign a professional contract. Duke University, one of a select group of institutions that accepted fewer than one out of ten applicants, routinely enrolled first-year basketball players who never reached their second year: The experience became known as "one and done."

Admissions scandals, parents willing to risk jail to get their children into "prestigious, elite, select institutions," universities eager to boost exclusivity even as they reject 90 percent or more of their applicants, often predatory sexual misconduct with students by faculty and staff, student debt over a trillion dollars, a growing list of financially unstable colleges certain to fail in the near future— these are the stories that confront us routinely. Why wouldn't the average American despair? Is this a higher education "system" in an unstoppable decline?

28. *Some Observations on American Education* (Cambridge: Cambridge University Press, 1956), 63.

The Future of Higher Education in America

"In higher education, 'made in America' still is the finest label. My only advice is to add 'handle with care,' lest we too descend to the level of most other American industrial performance."

—HENRY ROSOVSKY[1]

In 1994 Clark Kerr, then eighty-three, gathered his thoughts about a century nearly ended and took on the challenge of attempting to anticipate the future. He himself had been an early casualty in the campus culture wars, having been dismissed in 1967 by Governor Ronald Reagan from the presidency of the University of California system because of perceived leniency in the face of student unrest. In *Troubled Times for American Higher Education: The 1990s and Beyond*, Kerr presented himself with an unanswerable question: "Why are we always so

1. "Highest Education," *New Republic*, July 13–20, 1987, 13–14.

happy looking backward and so unhappy looking forward? I do not fully understand."[2]

We should have no illusions when examining American higher education about how we evolved and where we find ourselves today. There is a measure of truth in each of the most brutal characterizations—and caricatures—that we find of our colleges and universities. As we face the third decade of the twenty-first century, there are a few facts about American higher education that cannot be denied.

RANGE OF CHOICE: AN ENDOWED PUBLIC AND PRIVATE UNIVERSE

There is no governing principle in American higher education. What we have is not "a system." The National Center for Educational Statistics lists over 1600 public degree-granting institutions and nearly 2000 nonprofit, private post-secondary colleges and universities, as well as more than 1000 for-profit universities. There is no controlling federal authority over faculty, curriculum, or governance. Applicants from all over the country may choose from a list of institutions that includes Harvard, Stanford, Hillsdale, Oral Roberts, Eastern Nazarene, Dade County Community College, the University of Michigan, Georgia Tech, Morehouse,

2. Clark Kerr, in association with Marian L. Gade and Maureen Kawaoka, *Troubled Times for American Education: The 1990s and Beyond* (Albany: State University of New York Press, 1994), 183.

Moody Bible College, South Dakota Wesleyan, Baylor, Swarthmore, Wellesley, and thousands of other similar or different institutions. They may be urban or rural; tiny, with fewer than 100 students, or enormous, with more than 80,000; private or public; nonprofit or for-profit; secular or faith-based, two-year or four-year. No such variety of choice exists in any other country, and this extraordinary complexity is beyond replication.

Nor is there a comparable culture of charitable giving anywhere else on this planet. Approximately 1.5 million public charities, private foundations, and other types of nonprofit organizations in the United States channel nearly $400 billion of annual giving by Americans to their preferred charitable institutions; colleges and universities get approximately $50 billion of that amount from private or corporate philanthropic giving every year. The American nonprofit institutions collectively possess endowments of over $500 billion, with the top twenty-five alone enjoying more than half of the total. Four out of the top five endowments are at private institutions: Harvard ($40 billion), Yale ($30 billion), the University of Texas ($27 billion), Stanford ($27 billion), and Princeton ($26 billion). Since the end of World War II, college and university presidents have spent less time on academic governance as their commitment to fundraising has increased. The position of provost was created in the 1950s to provide a second university-wide academic authority, as the presidents' responsibilities often took them off the campus.

CAN IT BE EXPLAINED?
THE AMERICAN COLLEGE EXPERIENCE

In most every other country of the industrialized, developed world, decisions on who would be going on to university and what they would be studying are made when the candidates are between the ages of eleven and fifteen. The decision-makers are the state and the family. For most of these students, careers are decided on, and the secondary school system creates the appropriate pathway to implement these decisions. There is little waste and clear roads ahead, and the university experience, for those who attend, is one that concentrates exclusively on the chosen career. The students undergo an intensive and selective high school preparation: "lycée" in France, "Gymnasium" in Germany, "grammar school" in Great Britain; in China a student's score in the National Higher Education Entrance Examination—the gaokao—is the primary consideration for admission into university. Students then commence their university career training in a specific discipline. The career path is straight and generally uninterrupted. The appropriate documentation of attendance and accomplishment guarantees admission into the national university system. The state, federal, or regional government manages the schools and the universities. The teachers are civil servants.

In every other advanced developed nation, there are a handful of private universities, some with a Protestant or Catholic tradition, and a few that are the equivalent of private American business or law schools. They are embedded in a governing system of education that from the lowest grades is controlled and funded by the state.

In the United States there is no such organizing principle. More than 13,000 local school boards direct the public education from K to 12, and accredited private schools offer opportunities for parents to choose an alternative to what comes next in education. While career paths may exist for some, the door remains wide open for most students: This institution called "college" delays career choices for four more years for millions of adolescents, creating an escape from real-world decisions. Millions of American college applicants select "undecided" as the career choice on their post-secondary applications. Most institutions do not require a decision about an academic major until either the second or third year of study. You may enter "medicine" at the start, but you may emerge as a student of comparative religion on your way to a divinity school. Or you might still become a physician. American medical schools require eight to ten "indicator courses"—two years of chemistry through organic, a year of biology, a year of physics, a semester or year of calculus—and then the budding physician can feel free to major in classics, theatre, ancient history, or any of the myriad choices available to most American undergraduates in college. Unless they have selected a business college or a similar institution with a more focused curriculum, these students—generally between the ages of seventeen and twenty-one, and still seeing pediatricians for their medical care—have available a wide range of elective courses that expose them to subjects they previously might never have examined. Even the most rigorous science program requires a broad background in the arts, social sciences, and humanities to go along with the "major" field of study, after four years of this, one "commences." This final event is called "commencement," which is actually what it says: the beginning. Perhaps one out of three matriculants in an American liberal arts college stays on the career choice path chosen at the beginning; for two out of three, it may be years before they find their genuine vocation. It is an education for changing one's mind and career direction once, twice, or more. For better or worse, there is nothing like it in the world.

COLLEGIATE ATHLETICS

This is another example of American exceptionalism in higher education, in the form of a self-inflicted wound. There is nothing in the world like the American appetite for collegiate football and basketball athletic competition at the premier level called Division I. An enormous body of documentation shows the abuses and exploitation of talented athletes for the commercial benefits of a small number of universities and the gratification of enthusiastic alumni. As hard as the apologists try to market the idea of "scholar-athletes," the result has been a system with no relationship to any educational or research mission of the institution.[3] The disconnect between these activities and what universities do regarding teaching, learning, and research is total. It represents an American obsession with sports and gambling, with huge profits accruing to both commercial entities—manufacturing equipment, clothing, or other sports-related parapher-nalia—and a handful of universities willing to participate. Other countries share our obsessions with sports and gambling, but none of them use their academic institu-tions as the vehicle to promote them. Reform has been futile. For decades, various organizations have pointed to the exploitation of these athletes who are alleged to be students. Two monolithic enterprises prevent any mean-ingful change: the gambling empire that radiates from Las Vegas across the nation, fueling the American ad-diction, and the National Collegiate Athletic Association in Indianapolis, the ostensible intercollegiate regulatory agency that itself has become a billion-dollar partner

3. There are many excellent, scholarly, and readable sources. Any-thing written by Andrew Zimbalist can be recommended. I suggest *Un-paid Professionals: Commercialism and Conflict in Big-Time College Sports* (Princeton: Princeton University Press, 1999), which was soon followed by James L. Shulman and William G. Bowen, *The Game of Life: College Sports and Educational Values* (Princeton: Princeton University Press, 2001). More strident but still reliable and academic is Murray Sperber, *Beer and Circus: How Big-Time College Sports Is Crippling Undergradu-ate Education* (New York: Henry Holt, 2000). John U. Bacon, a sports journalist, concentrates on football in *Fourth and Long: The Fight for the Soul of College Football* (New York: Simon and Schuster, 2013). One of hundreds of articles is Neil Swidey's cover article "College Sports Is Broken," *Boston Globe Magazine*, May 19, 2019.

through its control of enormous television contracts that fuel the gambling activities. With the Internet and online gambling, the scale of gambling operations has become even more staggering. The University of Michigan athletic department projected for the year 2020 operating revenues of $196.3 million. The payout for the football television contact alone was $56 million.[4] No authority knows how much is bet both legally and illegally on college sports in the United States, but online estimates *start* at $100 *billion* annually.

This is not a recent development. Only the scale has grown. Intercollegiate sports as mass entertainment with commercial significance began at the University of Chicago when its football coach, Amos Alonzo Stagg, was given a lifetime appointment as professor of physical culture in 1892.[5] The big collegiate stadiums soon followed, and journalists have fully documented for the past seventy years the narrative of the contemporary abuses of bribery, debasement of academic standards for athletes, and general corruption by sports companies seeking endorsements of their products and gamblers pursuing college players to fix games.[6] College basketball has

4. Angelique S. Chengelis, "Michigan's Big Ten Payout Expected to Increase to $56 Million, Warde Manuel Says," *Detroit News*, June 20, 2019, https://www.detroitnews.com/story/sports/college/university-michigan/2019/06/20/michigans-big-ten-payout-expected-increase-56-million-warde-manuel-says/1509550001/.

5. See Robin Lester, *Stagg's University: The Rise, Decline, and Fall of Big-Time Football at Chicago* (Champaign: University of Illinois Press, 1999).

6. The City College of New York basketball point-shaving scandal of 1949–50 became a national story that brought public attention to the

been added to the mix and now the event known as March Madness, when the NCAA-designated Division I conference winners play off in a weeks-long competition to select the national champion, has become a billion-dollar gambling event, among the largest in the world. At least two of the basketball coaches of the final four participants in 2019 were earning more than $4 million a year.[7]

Despite the regularly occurring sports scandals and the exploitation of collegiate athletes, there is no national will to reform the current state of affairs.[8] The commercial grip, the public's enthusiastic endorsement, and profits for selective universities are too powerful to expect any change.[9]

---

vulnerability of college basketball when gamblers could bribe players. See Stanley Cohen, *The Game They Played* (New York: Carroll & Graf, 2001). Nothing has changed. See Billy Witz, "Cash-Filled Shoe Box and Other Ploys Are Detailed at Corruption Trial," *New York Times*, April 26, 2019, B10.

7. Football coaches account for the largest number of million-dollar salaries, but compensation for basketball coaches does not lag far behind. See Marc Tracy, *New York Times*, "Louisiana State's $2.5 Million Man Isn't Even the Head Coach," October 12, 2018; Doug Lederman, "27 College Football Coaches Make More Than $3 Million," *Inside Higher Education*, November 20, 2014.

8. The most comprehensive study of efforts to reform is John R. Thelin, *Games Colleges Play: Scandal and Reform in Intercollegiate Athletics* (Baltimore: Johns Hopkins University Press, 1994).

9. See Joshua Hunt, *University of Nike: How Corporate Cash Bought American Higher Education* (Brooklyn, N.Y.: Melville House, 2018). The best minds in American higher education have made efforts, but to no avail. See William G. Bowen and Sarah A. Levin, *Reclaiming the Game: College Sports and Educational Values* (Princeton: Princeton University Press, 2003). For the NCAA grip, see Jake New, "NCAA Reaches $8.8 Billion Broadcast Deal," *Inside Higher Education*, April 13, 2016. Most of the daily newspapers still printing carry the Las Vegas point spreads during the collegiate football and basketball seasons.

THE KING IS DEAD, LONG LIVE THE NEXT KING: CHINA?

China will overtake the US in ten years, China's win is unstoppable.

—ZHAO LIJIAN, Chinese Foreign Ministry, quoted in the *Wall Street Journal,* 2019[10]

In the *Wall Street Journal* (June 25, 2019), Richard K. Vedder's book *Restoring the Promise: Higher Education in America*[11] was reviewed by Allen C. Guelzo. Both had long faculty careers and shared the belief that American colleges and universities were "overpriced caricatures, bloated, irrelevant, and in decline, producing over-educated baristas . . . in vacuous classes with inflated grading . . . a dinosaur—an overbuilt, under-achieving creature whose chances of survival are increasingly dim."[12] When it comes crashing down, says Guelzo, "it will help bring to a close an era that [Vedder] has, rightly, come to deplore."

As I have been suggesting, such criticism of American higher education has been a growth industry for most of the postwar decades. Inevitably, the anticipated failure has been associated with the rise and triumph of other

10. Charles Hutzler, "China's Growing Power, and a Growing Backlash," *Wall Street Journal*, December 18, 2019, R13.

11. Richard K. Vedder, *Restoring the Promise: Higher Education in America* (Oakland: Independent Institute, 2019).

12. Allen C. Guelzo, "High Cost, Low Yield," Wall Street Journal, June 25, 2019, A15.

nations' higher education establishments: The Soviet Union in the Sputnik era, the European Union, Japan, and now China. Although none of the challengers were able to shove the American higher education enterprise off its dominant perch, many American voices now assure the world that China will be the next dominant force in research and scientific achievement.

This author lacks any credible expertise to determine China's capacity to take global higher education leadership from the United States. In spite of the relentless criticism, by every measure available, the American research universities continue to lead the world as we enter the third decade of the twenty-first century. The opportunity to spend two years at community college, or four in an undergraduate college or university, remains unique and attractive for anyone who can afford a campus experience—in spite of the maddening irrelevance of athletic activities among a small number of schools and the almost implausible diversity of the mostly ungoverned higher education enterprise. Whatever Congressional restrictions and presidential executive degrees may accomplish in making an American education more difficult to attain for international students, no other country has yet attracted the number of visitors who come to our campuses. The extraordinary reach of the English language, unprecedented in world history, has made this possible.[13] One in four people around the globe speaks English; 20 percent of books published

13. Gaston Dorren, *Babel: Around the World in Twenty Languages* (New York: Atlantic Monthly, 2018).

worldwide are in English; over 80 percent of scholarly articles are written in English. Only machine translation and artificial intelligence in a much more perfected state, the so-called Babel Chip, could alter this reality.[14]

There is no shortage of experts or opinions on China's rise in the last forty years and its aspirations to surpass the United States as an economic, military, and educational global leader. The sheer size of the Chinese economic revolution since the 1980s under Deng Xiaoping and more recently Xi Jinping is impressive. The number of Chinese higher educational institutions grew from 598 universities in 1978 to 2,100 in 2012. The economic model of freewheeling capitalism under the control of a strict one-party state is China's public face.[15] The ruling Communist party hopes to present China as a durable and reliable future leader of the world. Some futurists agree; others do not. One side depicts the enormous economic progress: the building out of great cities such as Shanghai, the phenomenal disappearance of poverty from a huge part of the population, and China's eclipsing of Japan in the second decade of the twenty-first century as an economic powerhouse, trailing only the United States in the world economy. The Chinese universities' research

14. "We could imagine China outpacing the United States in the global education marketplace, especially if machine translation reduces the Chinese language barrier." Bryan Alexander, *Academia Next: The Futures of Higher Education* (Baltimore: Johns Hopkins University Press, 2020), 215.

15. See Dexter Roberts, *The Myth of Chinese Capitalism: The Worker, the Factory, and the Future of the World* (New York: St. Martin's, 2020), and Jonathan E. Hillman, *The Emperor's New Road: China and the Project of the Century* (New Haven: Yale University Press, 2020).

labs have undoubtedly contributed to the high-tech and high-speed expansion of Chinese efforts to dominate the Internet.

Recently the response to what our government sees as illegal incursions into American research space has been forceful. The Chinese began a recruitment program in 2008 called Thousand Talents, intending to attract Chinese diaspora scientists back home and bring their research with them. For many of the scientists, it became easier to access the hundreds of millions of dollars from this Chinese funding source than to compete for increasingly difficult NIH and NSF grants. The U.S. federal government saw the Chinese initiative as illegal theft of intellectual property and scientific knowledge. What had been a free flow of ideas across scientific communities around the world was dramatically interrupted by the arrest in January 2020 of Charles M. Lieber, a Harvard professor charged with making false statements to the U.S. government about receiving research funding from China. Lieber was marched off in leg irons and handcuffs. This is not the image to which American scientists committed to free exchange of ideas and openness are accustomed.[16]

This may prove to be an isolated event, and not a government policy that likely would affect research profoundly in this country. China is still not the United States. And yet, China has a billion-dollar higher education market in which academic competition, marred by

16. See Ellen Barry and Gina Kolata, ""China's Lavish Funds Lured U.S. Scientists. What Did It Get in Return?," *New York Times*, February 6, 2020, A12.

cheating and fraud is built into the culture. Thousands of dubious patents are awarded to Chinese students building college-worthy credentials, and plagiarism is rampant throughout the system.[17] The extraordinary competition for university seats produced over a billion students educated in mainland China in the past few decades, yet of the four ethnic Chinese Nobel Prize winners in science since World War II, two had done their research in the United States. President Xi Jinping has spoken of his desire to turn the country's university campuses into "strongholds of the Communist Party's Leadership."[18] Basic science research could suffer from a heavy hand.

Can this China serve as a model for global higher education in the future? In 2015 China ranked last of sixty-five nations in Internet freedom.[19] It is using every means at its disposal to control the spread of organized religion. Can a free and unhindered research environment exist in China?[20] Will a nation with that much state control attract faculty from other countries capable of the kind of freewheeling basic research and independence that

17. Some authors attempt to strike a balance in describing China's rise. See Yong Zhao, *Who's Afraid of the Big Bad Dragon? Why China Has the Best (and Worst) Education System in the World* (San Francisco: Jossey-Bass, 2014).

18. Douglas Belkin and Philip Wen, "American Colleges Wary of China Moves," *Wall Street Journal*, December 28–29, 2019, A3.

19. Freedom House, "Privatizing Censorship, Eroding Privacy: Freedom on the Net 2015," freedomhouse.org.

20. See Carl Minzner, *End of An Era: How China's Authoritarian Revival is Undermining Its Rise* (New York: Oxford University Press, 2018).

produced the 150 Nobel Prizes that immigrants earned on behalf of the United States?[21]

The Chinese and American models are different in almost every respect, but none as obvious as academic freedom: a state-controlled and operated university system of more or less similar institutions versus an independent, often ungovernable faculty who, even in grim times of cutbacks, scandals, and fewer positions, pretty much do things their own way.

THE AUTHENTIC AMERICAN EXCEPTION:
HIGHER EDUCATION

As of this writing, the world is wrestling with the public health crisis caused by the COVID-19 coronavirus, which began in China. Futurists who saw China as the new world leader in research and technology are having to examine how powerful central control and suppression of criticism that is built into a repressive system can expose a nation's intellectual weakness. For all our waste, scandals, athletic excesses, condemnations of political correctness, and pampering of students, our colleges and universities would be the strongest antidote to any government's efforts to hide a public health disaster. As one

21. The rapid spread of the coronavirus from China around the world revealed the Chinese government's inability to deal with a public health issue that can become a global health crisis. The World Health Organization on January 30, 2020, declared a global health emergency. Suddenly the People's Republic became a pariah, its citizens quarantined around the world, before lockdowns were instituted elsewhere.

observer noted, "China's mishandling of the coronavirus outbreak has imperiled itself and the world because it is a land of 21st-century science and 19th-century politics."[22]

Could an American president upend it all? If the Vannevar Bush model—massive federal support for basic research, with few strings controlling where the scientists take us—were assaulted, could American research dominance be toppled? Apparently the Congress has said no to that possibility. President Trump's 2020 federal budget called for a $2.6 billion cut in the NIH funding. The previous year, he had requested a $4.9 billion cut. But Congress, deeply divided on every other issue, increased the NIH funding by nearly 7 percent.[23] Federal support for financial aid may disappear, but basic research—and military spending—is above any partisan squabbles.

We may never be the "nation of educated people" that the economist and university president Howard Bowen had hoped for.[24] Anti-intellectualism runs too deeply through too many Americans to attain that national status. It is not surprising that our colleges and universities lack the respect of the nation. In the century since American scientific accomplishments outdistanced the rest of the world, our inclination to place the blame on higher education institutions and their faculty has only gotten

22. Nicholas Kristof, "'I Cannot Remain Silent'," *New York Times,* February 16, 2020, 9.

23. Gabriel T. Rubin, "Washington Wire," *Wall Street Journal*, February 15–16, 2020, A4.

24. *The State of the Nation and the Agenda for Higher Education* (San Francisco: Jossey-Bass, 1982).

stronger and become more widespread, even while we lead in discoveries and international recognition.[25]

Those authentically American characteristics of our campuses will not go away. Big-time intercollegiate athletics and the lure of billions of dollars will only grow larger and more inviting. Research universities seeking prestige will continue to produce twice as many Ph.D.s as the country can employ. Groups will battle for control of what they each consider the meaning of academic freedom, the American historical narrative, and the never-ending accusations of political correctness. What Clark Kerr in the 1990s called "troubled times for American higher education" will not go away, because Americans—having discovered that our colleges and universities are actually central to who we are and to what kind of nation we've become—won't let it. Politically conservative and liberally progressive Americans blame each other for imposing their versions of virtue and the good society on the campus, and have made it the battle-ground. We will not return to the days of President Wagstaff and the Gipper. But despite the enormous volume of critical writing and data suggesting that we are a country whose faculty and students are in academic decline, the successor to the singular accomplishment of American higher education is still not in sight. And may never be.

25. See Dennis Overbye, "In Battle of Giant Telescopes, Outlook for the U.S. Dims," *New York Times*, December 31, 2019, D6. The theme is decline: "Now, as the wheels of the academic and government bureaucracy begin to turn, many American astronomers worry that they are following in the footsteps of their physicist colleagues."

Acknowledgments

When writing a book about education as you approach your ninetieth year, you had better thank everyone who got you here and mention what was important; having confessed my age, there is no need to apologize for the inevitable omissions to the list: failing memory provides automatic forgiveness. So, here goes . . . Ms. Thorn in the seventh grade taught me how to diagram sentences, explained direct and indirect objects, and always reminded me: spelling and grammar count. My home room teacher at Memorial High School, Ms. Roslyn Sokel, made me take her typing class, then gave me my only C, because I wouldn't take my eyes off the keys, but I learned a valuable skill. Her close friend was Eileen O'Connor, my English teacher for four years, who punished me by making me confront Thackeray's *Vanity Fair*, the first novel I ever read, when I punched William Goska through her classroom closet. My high school baseball coach Mr.

Bocchieri picked my "university," a mostly Methodist seminary with a tiny liberal arts college—and a baseball team—not far from my home, which suited my parents, who didn't want their baby far away. At Drew my Methodist minister teacher Heisse Johnson taught me how to read the Hebrew Bible and the Christian Bible, as he called them. Sherman Plato Young, another minister, made me read all of the Greek tragedies and called Clytemnestra "the original hatchet woman." John Schabacker, who wasn't even a Methodist, was the entire German department and introduced me to the wonder of German prepositions, literature, history great or horrible—and put me on a career path. At Michigan, there was Otto Graf, who mentored young graduate students and their spouses. As a colleague, there was no better teacher than Sylvan Barnet. Most grateful thanks to Tufts Dean Charles Stearns, who placed his hands on my head and pronounced that henceforth I was a tenured faculty member. To these mentors, I owe everything.

I have a special debt to my students at Tufts over more than fifty years. The earliest ones, many now retired, have remained lifelong learners and friends who after their commencement kept teaching me and themselves: Susan Pauker, Jim Fratello, John McCarthy, Steve Wermiel, Jim Stern, Phil Primack, Judy Mears, Tom Glynn, Nancy Goodman, Barbara Harman, David Chase, Jon Charry, Peter Skerry, Frank Siteman, Bill Purves, David Frankel, Lloyd Zuckerberg, Nadine Brozan, Mark Pomar, Ed Dente, Connie Schwartz, Jeanne Hambright Moore, Fran Putnoi, Paul Taskier, and all the Massarottis. Jeremy

Wang-Iverson, a younger one still working, took charge of this manuscript when I grew tired. There are many others, right up to my retirement, who have my thanks and gratitude.

Career changes had a profound impact. I was greatly fortunate that Nathan Gantcher quit dental school, Jim Stern moved away from engineering, Steve Manos abandoned the practice of law, and Dan Barber did more than just bake bread. They made wise choices, from which Tufts—and I—have profoundly benefitted. Great friendships are irreplaceable.

The Tisch Library staff at Tufts University, particularly Amey Callahan and Chris Barbour, cared for my every bibliographic need. David Bragg, who took pity on the technologically challenged elderly, patiently guided my way. My granddaughter Celia fetched and carried book after book.

To all of you, and to many more: my deepest gratitude.

SG

Index

ABOUT THE AUTHOR

Sol Gittleman is the Alice and Nathan Gantcher University Professor Emeritus at Tufts University, where he taught from 1964 until his retirement in 2015. He served as provost from 1981 to 2002 and has received many awards, fellowships, and honorary degrees for his teaching and service.